Experiencing Architecture

P9-CMV-056

Andreas Feininger: New York

Experiencing
Architecture

by Steen Eiler Rasmussen

The M. I. T. Press

Massachusetts Institute of Technology

CAMBRIDGE

Second printing, October 1962

Third printing, first MIT Press paperback edition,
February 1964

Fourth printing, October 1964

Fifth printing, March 1966

Sixth printing, February 1967

Seventh printing, October 1968

Eighth printing, February 1970

Ninth printing, November 1972

Tenth printing, April 1973

Eleventh printing, November 1973

Twelfth printing, March 1974

ISBN 0 262 18003 0 (hardcover)

ISBN 0 262 68002 5 (paperback)

Library of Congress Catalog Card Number 62–21637

Printed in the United States of America

Contents

Preface

When my previous book, "Towns and Buildings," appeared the learned English historian of architecture, John Summerson, wrote that the preface should have contained some reference to whom the book was written for. The reader should have been warned so that he would avoid being disappointed and annoyed when he discovered how elementary the book actually was. Therefore I now hasten to state that I have endeavored to write the present volume in such a way that even an interested teen-ager might understand it. Not because I expect to find many readers belonging to that age-group. But if it can be understood by a fourteen-year-old then certainly it will be understood by those who are older. Furthermore, there is also some hope that the author himself has understood what he has written—which the reader is by no means always convinced of when reading books on art. *Oh, how true!*

In writing this volume I naturally hope that my architect colleagues will read it and that they will find something of interest in the thoughts and ideas I have gathered during many years. But the book has a further aim. I believe that it is important to tell people outside our profession what it is that we are engaged in. In olden days the entire community took part in forming the dwellings and implements they used. The individual was in fruitful contact with these things; the anonymous houses were built with a natural feeling for place, materials and use and the result was a remarkably suitable comeliness. Today, in our highly civilized society the houses which ordinary people are doomed to live in and gaze upon are on the whole without quality. We cannot, however, go back to the old method of personally supervised handicrafts. We must strive to advance by arousing interest in and understanding of the work the architect does. The basis of competent professionalism is a sympathetic and knowledgeable group of amateurs, of non-professional art-lovers. It is not my intention to attempt to teach people what is right or wrong, what is beautiful or ugly. I regard all art as a means of expression and that which may be right for one artist may well be wrong for another. My object is in all modesty to endeavor to explain the instrument the architect plays on, to show what a great range it has and thereby awaken the senses to its music. But even though I do not propose to pass æsthetic judgments, it is very difficult to hide one's likes and dislikes. If one wants to demonstrate the instrument of an art it is not enough to explain its mechanics as a physicist would. One must, as it were, play a tune on it so that the hearer gets an idea of what it can do—and in such case is it possible to avoid putting emphasis and feeling into the performance?

The present volume is about how we perceive things that surround us and it has proved difficult to find the right words for this. More than in any other book, I have struggled with my material in the attempt to formulate it simply and clearly, working it over and over again. But all my exertion would undoubtedly have been unavailing if I had not had illustrations to support the text. Therefore, I would like to thank the Ny Carlsberg Foundation for its help which made the illustrative material possible. I also am greatly indebted to my publishers. That the book has appeared at all is due to the encouragement of Dean Pietro Belluschi of M.I.T. and The M.I.T. Press in Cambridge, Massachusetts. It has been a pleasure to work in close co-operation with Mrs. Eve Wendt who made the translation from Danish and did it so well that I feel that my American and British friends should recognize my voice when reading this book. I am glad to have here an opportunity to express my sincere thanks to her. I also remember with gratitude the pleasant and fruitful co-operation with my friends the printers and the block-makers.

Steen Eiler Rasmussen.

CHAPTER I

Basic Observations

For centuries architecture, painting and sculpture have been called the Fine Arts, that is to say the arts which are concerned with "the beautiful" and appeal to the eye, just as music appeals to the ear. And indeed most people judge architecture by its external appearance, just as books on the subject are usually illustrated with pictures of building exteriors.

When an architect judges a building its appearance is only one of several factors which interest him. He studies plans, sections and elevations and maintains that, if it is to be a good building, these must harmonize with each other. Just what he means by this is not easy to explain. At any rate, not everyone can understand it any more than everyone can visualize a building merely by looking at the plans. A man to whom I was explaining a project for a house he wanted to build, said deprecatingly: "I really *don't like* sections." He was a rather delicate person and I got the impression that the mere idea of cutting into anything was repulsive to him. But his reluctance may have arisen from the correct idea of architecture as something indivisible, something you cannot separate into a number of elements. Architecture is not produced simply by adding plans and sections to elevations. It is something else and something more. It is impossible to explain precisely what it is—its limits are by no means well-defined. On the whole, art should not be explained; it must be experienced. But by means of words it is possible to help others to experience it, and that is what I shall attempt to do here.

The architect works with form and mass just as the sculptor does, and like the painter he works with color. But alone of the three, his is a functional art. It solves practical problems. It creates tools or implements for human beings and utility plays a decisive role in judging it.

Architecture is a very special functional art; it confines space so we can dwell in it, creates the framework around our lives. In other words, the difference between sculpture and architecture is not that the former is concerned with more organic forms, the latter with more abstract. Even the most abstract piece of sculpture, limited to purely geometric shapes, does not become architecture. It lacks a decisive factor: utility.

The master photographer, Andreas Feininger, has taken a picture showing a cemetery in the Brooklyn-Queens area of New York. The tombstones stand crowded together exactly like skyscrapers in an American city, the very skyscrapers which form the distant background of the photograph.

Seen from an aeroplane high in the air, even the most gigantic skyscraper is only a tall stone block, a mere sculptural form, not a real building in which people can live. But as the plane descends from the great heights there will be one moment when the buildings change character completely. Suddenly they take on human scale, become houses for human beings like ourselves, not the tiny dolls observed from the heights. This strange transformation takes place at the instant when the contours of the buildings begin to rise above the horizon so that we get a side view of them instead of looking down on them. The buildings pass into a new stage of existence, become architecture in place of neat toys—for architecture means shapes formed around man, formed to be lived in, not merely to be seen from the outside.

The architect is a sort of theatrical producer, the man who plans the setting for our lives. Innumerable circumstances are dependent on the way he arranges this setting for us. When his intentions succeed, he is like the perfect host who provides every comfort for his guests so that living with him is a happy experience. But his producer job is difficult for several reasons. First of all, the actors are quite ordinary people. He must be aware of their natural way of acting; otherwise the whole thing will be a fiasco. That which may be quite right and natural in one cultural environment can easily be wrong in another; what is fitting and

proper in one generation becomes ridiculous in the next when
people have acquired new tastes and habits. This is clearly
demonstrated by the picture of the Danish Renaissance king,

Christian IV—as interpreted by a popular Danish actor—
riding a bicycle. The costume, of its kind, is undoubtedly a
handsome one, and the bicycle too is of the best. But they simply
do not go together. In the same way, it is impossible to take over
the beautiful architecture of a past era; it becomes false and
pretentious when people can no longer live up to it.

The 19th century had the very ill-advised idea that to obtain the best results it was necessary only to copy fine old buildings that were universally admired. But when in a modern city you build a modern office building with a façade that is a faithful copy of a Venetian palace, it becomes quite meaningless even though its prototype is charming—charming, that is, in Venice on the right site and in the right surroundings.

Another great difficulty is that the architect's work is intended to live on into a distant future. He sets the stage for a long, slowmoving performance which must be adaptable enough to accommodate unforeseen improvisations. His building should preferably be ahead of its time when planned so that it will be in keeping with the times as long as it stands.

The architect also has something in common with the landscape gardener. Everyone can grasp the fact that the gardener's success depends on whether or not the plants he selects for the garden thrive there. No matter how beautiful his conception of a garden may be it will, nevertheless, be a failure if it is not the right environment for the plants, if they cannot flourish in it. The architect, too, works with living things—with human beings, who are much more incalculable than plants. If they cannot thrive in his house its apparent beauty will be of no avail—without life it becomes a monstrosity. It will be neglected, fall into disrepair and change into something quite different from what he intended. Indeed, one of the proofs of good architecture is that it is being utilized as the architect had planned.

Finally, there is a very important feature which must not be overlooked in any attempt to define the true nature of architecture. That is the creative process, how the building comes into existence. Architecture is not produced by the artist himself as, for instance, paintings are.

A painter's sketch is a purely personal document; his brush stroke is as individual as his hand-writing; an imitation of it is a forgery. This is not true of architecture. The architect remains anonymously in the background. Here again he resembles the

Palazzo Vendramin-Calergi, Venice. Completed 1509

23 Havnegade, Copenhagen. Completed 1865. Architect F. Meldahl

theatrical producer. His drawings are not an end in themselves, a work of art, but simply a set of instructions, an aid to the craftsmen who construct his buildings. He delivers a number of completely impersonal plan drawings and typewritten specifications. They must be so unequivocal that there will be no doubt about the construction. He composes the music which others will play. Furthermore, in order to understand architecture fully, it must be remembered that the people who play it are not sensitive musicians interpreting another's score—giving it special phrasing, accentuating one thing or another in the work. On the contrary, they are a multitude of ordinary people who, like ants toiling together to build an ant-hill, quite impersonally contribute their particular skills to the whole, often without understanding that which they are helping to create. Behind them is the architect who organizes the work, and architecture might well be called an art of organization. The building is produced like a motion picture without star performers, a sort of documentary film with ordinary people playing all the parts.

Compared with other branches of art, all this may seem quite negative; architecture is incapable of communicating an intimate, personal message from one person to another; it entirely lacks emotional sensitivity. But this very fact leads to something positive. The architect is forced to seek a form which is more explicit and finished than a sketch or personal study. Therefore, architecture has a special quality of its own and great clarity. The fact that rhythm and harmony have appeared at all in architecture —whether a medieval cathedral or the most modern steel-frame building—must be attributed to the organization which is the underlying idea of the art.

No other art employs a colder, more abstract form, but at the same time no other art is so intimately connected with man's daily life from the cradle to the grave.

Architecture is produced by ordinary people, for ordinary people; therefore it should be easily comprehensible to all. It is based on a number of human instincts, on discoveries and ex-

periences common to all of us at a very early stage in our lives
—above all, our relation to inanimate things. This can perhaps
best be illustrated by comparison with animals.

Certain natural capacities with which many animals are born,
man acquires only by patient endeavor. It takes years for a
small child to learn to stand, to walk, to jump, to swim. On the
other hand, the human being very soon extends his mastery to
include things which are apart from himself. With the help of
all kinds of implements he develops his efficiency and enlarges
his scope of action in a way no animal can emulate.

In his helplessness, the baby begins by tasting things, touching
them, handling them, crawling on them, toddling over them, to
find out what they are like, whether friendly or hostile. But
he quickly learns to use all sorts of contrivances and thereby
avoids some of the more unpleasant experiences.

Soon the child becomes quite adept in the employment of
these things. He seems to project his nerves, all his senses, deep
into the lifeless objects. Confronted by a wall which is so high
that he cannot reach up to feel the top, he nevertheless obtains

Boys playing a ball game on the top step of the stairway behind the church of S. Maria Maggiore in Rome (1952)

an impression of what it is like by throwing his ball against it. In this way he discovers that it is entirely different from a tautly stretched piece of canvas or paper. With the help of the ball he receives an impression of the hardness and solidity of the wall.

The enormous church of S. Maria Maggiore stands on one of Rome's seven famous hills. Originally the site was very unkempt, as can be seen in an old fresco painting in the Vatican. Later, the slopes were smoothed and articulated with a flight of steps up to the apse of the basilica. The many tourists who are brought to the church on sight-seeing tours hardly notice the unique character of the surroundings. They simply check off one of the starred numbers in their guide-books and hasten on to the next one. But they do not experience the place in the way some boys I saw there a few years ago did. I imagine they were pupils from a nearby monastery school. They had a recess at eleven o'clock

View from the top step behind S. Maria Maggiore, Rome (1952)

and employed the time playing a very special kind of ball game on the broad terrace at the top of the stairs. It was apparently a kind of football but they also utilized the wall in the game, as in squash—a curved wall, which they played against with great virtuosity. When the ball was *out*, it was most decidedly out, bouncing down all the steps and rolling several hundred feet further on with an eager boy rushing after it, in and out among motor cars and Vespas down near the great obelisk.

I do not claim that these Italian youngsters learned more about architecture than the tourists did. But quite unconsciously they experienced certain basic elements of architecture: the horizontal planes and the vertical walls above the slopes. And they learned to play on these elements. As I sat in the shade watching them, I sensed the whole three-dimensional composition as never before. At a quarter past eleven the boys dashed off, shouting and laughing. The great basilica stood once more in silent grandeur. In similar fashion the child familiarizes himself with all sorts of playthings which increase his opportunities to experience his surroundings. If he sucks his finger and sticks it in the air, he discovers what the wind is like in the low strata of air in which he moves about. But with a kite he has an aerial feeler out high up in the atmosphere. He is one with his hoop, his scooter, his bicycle. By a variety of experiences he quite instinctively learns to judge things according to weight, solidity, texture, heat-conducting ability.

Before throwing a stone he first gets the feel of it, turning it over and over until he has the right grip on it, and then weighing it in his hand. After doing this often enough, he is able to tell what a stone is like without touching it at all; a mere glance is sufficient.

When we see a spherical object we do not simply note its spherical shape. While observing it we seem to pass our hands over it in order to experience its various characteristics.

Though the many kinds of balls and marbles that are used in various games have the same geometric shape, we recognize them as objects of extremely different character. Their size alone, in relation to the human hand, not only gives them different quantities but different qualities. Color plays a part, but weight and strength are much more important. The large football, made to be kicked, is essentially different from the little white tennis ball that is struck by the hand, or by the racquet which is simply an extension of the hand.

At an early age the child discovers that some things are hard, others soft, and some so plastic that they can be kneaded and moulded by hand. He learns that the hard ones can be ground by still harder materials so that they become sharp and pointed, and therefore objects cut like a diamond are perceived as hard. Quite the reverse, pliable stuffs, like bread dough, can be given rounded forms, and no matter how you cut them up, the section will always show an unbroken curve.

Various balls used in English ball games

From such observations we learn that there are certain forms which are called hard and others soft, regardless of whether the materials they are made of are actually soft or hard.

As an example of a "soft" form in a hard material we can take a so-called pear-shaped cup from the English firm Wedgwood. It is an old model but it is impossible to say when the form first appeared. It is very alien to the classical shapes which the founder of the firm, Josiah Wedgwood, preferred to all others. It may be that it is of Persian ancestry and was permitted to live on in English guise because it suits the potter's craft so well. You feel that you can actually see how it was drawn up on the potter's wheel, how the soft clay humbly submitted to the hands of the potter, suffering itself to be pressed in below so that it could swell out above. The handle is not cast in a mould, as on most cups today, but formed with the fingers. To avoid rims, the plastic clay is squeezed out like toothpaste from a tube, shaped over the potter's fingers and then fixed to the cup in a slender curve which is pleasant to grasp. A man at the Wedgwood works, who sat making these handles, said to me that it was lovely work and that he enjoyed curving the handle in towards the pear-shaped cup. He knew no words for more complicated sensations; otherwise he might have said that he liked the rhythm in cup and handle. But though he could not express this, he had experienced it. When we say that such a cup has a "soft" form, it is entirely due to a series of experiences we gathered in childhood, which taught us how soft and hard materials respond to manipulation. Though the cup, after firing, is hard, we are nevertheless aware that it was soft at the time it was shaped.

In this instance we have a soft thing that was hardened by a special process, namely firing, and it is easy to understand why we continue to think of it as soft. But even in cases where the material used was hard from the very beginning, we can speak of soft forms. And this conception of soft and hard forms, acquired from objects small enough to handle, is applied even to the largest structures.

So-called pear-shaped cup manufactured by Wedgwood
The cup was soft when it was shaped; after firing the material became hard
but the form itself can still be described as soft

As a typical example of a structure with soft forms we can take an English bridge built at the beginning of the nineteenth century. It is obviously made of brick, that is of a material that was hard at the time the bridge was constructed. Nevertheless it is impossible to rid yourself of the impression of something that was kneaded and moulded, something that responded to pressure in the same way the banks of streams and rivers do, acquiring the form of winding curves as the rushing water carries off masses of clay and gravel from one bank and deposits it on the other. The bridge has a double function: it is a raised roadway and a navigation portal that seems to have been hollowed out by the pressure of running water.

As an example of the opposite quality, that is, a structure whose form is manifestly "hard", we select the Roman Palazzo Punta di Diamanti. Not only is the entire building mass a clearcut prism, but the lower part is made of stone with faceted

*Palazzo Punta
di Diamanti
in Rome.
A building with
a typically
"hard" form*

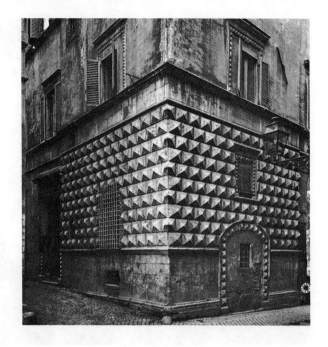

rusticationslike projecting pyramids—so-called diamond-shaped ashlar. Here, the detail has been directly taken over from a tiny object and employed on a much larger scale.

Certain periods have preferred hard effects of this kind while others have endeavored to make their buildings "soft," and there is much architecture which sets the soft against the hard for the sake of contrast.

Form can also give an impression of heaviness or lightness. A wall built of large stones, which we realize must have required great effort to bring to the site and put in place, appears heavy to us. A smooth wall seems light, even though it may have necessitated much harder work and actually weigh more than the stone wall. We intuitively feel that granite walls are heavier than brick ones without having any idea of their respective weights. Ashlar masonry with deep joints is often imitated in brick, not to produce a deception but simply as a means of artistic expression.

Impressions of hardness and softness, of heaviness and lightness, are connected with the surface character of materials. There
are innumerable kinds of surfaces from the coarsest to the finest.
If building materials were graded according to degrees of rough-
ness, there would be a great number of them with almost imper-
ceptible differences. At one end of the scale would be undressed
timber and pebble-dash, at the other polished stone and smoothly
varnished surfaces.

It may not be surprising that we can see such differences with
the naked eye but it is certainly remarkable that, without touching the materials, we are aware of the essential difference between
such things as fired clay, crystalline stone, and concrete.

In Denmark today sidewalks are often paved with several rows
of concrete slabs separated by rows of granite cobblestones. It is

undoubtedly practical, when necessary to lift the slab of concrete, to be able to rest the crowbar against the hard granite,
which is less likely to crumble. But the combination gives a
singularly inharmonious surface. Granite and concrete do not
mix well; you can almost feel how unpleasant it is right through
the soles of your shoes—the two materials are of such different
grades of smoothness. And when, as sometimes happens, this
pavement is flanked by broad strips of asphalt or gravel and edged
with kerbstone, the modern Danish sidewalk becomes a veritable sample collection of paving materials, not to be compared
with the pavements of more civilized eras, which are pleasing to
the eye and comfortable under foot. The Londoner calls his
sidewalk the "pavement," and a more cultivated example of
paving can hardly be found.

*Clinker paved
colonnade in
Copenhagen.
Heavy granite
column stands
directly on the
lighter paving
material,
shattering the
pattern of the
brick paving*

Cobblestone paved square in Fribourg, Switzerland

In Switzerland the cobblestone paving is exceedingly handsome, as can be seen in the photographs of a tranquil little square in Fribourg where the beautifully laid pavement gives æsthetic pleasure to the eye and has its perfect foil in the uniform pale yellow limestone of the surrounding walls and the fountain. A great variety of materials can be used for paving with very satisfactory results, but they cannot be combined or used arbitrarily. In Holland they use clinkers in the streets and on the highways and secure a neat and pleasant surface. But when the same material is used as a foundation for granite pillars, as in

Stormgade in Copenhagen, the effect is far from good. Not only do the clinkers become chipped, but you have the uncomfortable feeling that the heavy pillars are sinking into the softer material.

At about the time when the child becomes aware of the textures of various materials he also forms an idea of tautness as opposed to slackness. The boy who makes a bow and draws the string so tightly that it hums, enjoys its tautness and receives an impression for life of a tense curve and when he sees a fishing net hung up to dry, he experiences how reposeful its slack and heavy lines are.

Square in Fribourg, Switzerland. Paving seen from the terrace above

Fishing net hung up to dry in Venice
The swelling forms of domes seen through the pendent lines of the net

There are monumental structures of the greatest simplicity which produce only a single effect, such as hardness or softness. But most buildings consist of a combination of hard and soft, light and heavy, taut and slack, and of many kinds of surfaces. These are all elements of architecture, some of the things the architect can call into play. And to experience architecture, you must be aware of all of these elements.

*Every instrument
has its own
physiognomy.
The sight of a tennis
racquet provokes
a feeling of vitality*

From these individual qualities let us now turn to the things themselves.

When we regard the tools produced by man—using the term tools in the broad sense which includes buildings and their rooms —we find that by means of material, form, color and other perceptive qualities, man has been able to give each tool its individual character. Each one seems to have its own personality which fairly speaks to us like a helpful friend, a good comrade. And each implement has its own particular effect upon our minds.

In this way, man first puts his stamp on the implements he makes and thereafter the implements exert their influence on man. They become more than purely useful articles. Besides expanding our field of action, they increase our vitality. A tennis racquet can help us to strike a ball better than we can do with the hand alone. This, however, is not the most important thing about it. As a matter of fact, striking balls is in itself of no particular

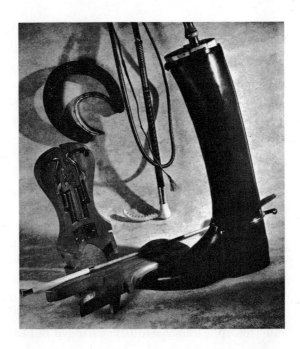

The English ridingboot has an aristocratic air and it produces an effect of costliness and elegance

value to anyone. But using the racquet gives us a feeling of being alive, fills us with energy and exuberance. The sight of it alone stimulates the tennis player in a way that is difficult to describe. But if we turn to another piece of sports equipment—the riding boot, for example,—we will immediately realize what different sensations the various things arouse. There is something aristocratic about an English riding boot. It's a rather odd-looking leather sheath, only faintly reminiscent of the shape of the human leg. It awakens sensations of elegance and luxury—calls to mind prancing thoroughbreds and pink coats. Or take the umbrella. It is an ingenious, thoroughly functional device, neat and practical. But you simply cannot imagine it in company with the racquet or the riding boot. They do not speak the same language. There seems to be something finicky about an umbrella, something rather cold and reserved—an air of dignity which the racquet utterly lacks.

We get to the point where we cannot describe our impressions of an object without treating it as a living thing with its own physiognomy. For even the most precise description, enumerating all visible characteristics, will not give an inkling of what we feel is the essence of the thing itself. Just as we do not notice the individual letters in a word but receive a total impression of the idea the word conveys, we generally are not aware of what it is that we perceive but only of the conception created in our minds when we perceive it.

Not only the tennis racquet but everything connected with the game—the court, the tennis player's clothes—arouses the same sensations. The garb is loose and comfortable, the shoes are soft—in keeping with the relaxed condition in which the player moves about the court idly picking up balls, reserving his energy for the speed and concentration which will be demanded of him the instant the ball is in play. If, later in the day, the same man appears at an official function in uniform or formal attire, not only his appearance will have changed but his entire being. His posture and gait are influenced by his clothes; restraint and dignity are now the keynote.

Turning from these examples from daily life to architecture, we find that the best buildings have been produced when the architect has been inspired by something in the problem which will give the building a distinctive stamp. Such buildings are created in a special spirit and they convey that spirit to others.

External features become a means of communicating feelings and moods from one person to another. Often, however, the only message conveyed is one of conformity. Man is less lonely when he feels that he is part of a general movement. People who get together for a common purpose try to appear as much alike as possible. If one of them finds himself a bit conspicuous, he is likely to feel miserable; the entire occasion is spoiled for him.

In pictures from a particular period people seem to look very much alike. It is not only a question of clothes and the style of hair-dress, but of posture and movement and the entire manner in which the people conduct themselves. In memoirs of the same period you find that the mode of living harmonizes with the external picture, and you will also find that the buildings, streets and towns were attuned to the rhythm of the era.

When it had passed historians discovered that a definite style had dominated the period and they gave it a name. But those who lived in that style were not aware of it. Whatever they did, however they dressed, seemed natural to them. We speak of a "Gothic" period or a "Baroque" period, and dealers in antiques and those who make their living manufacturing fake antiques are familiar with all the small details that are characteristic of each style in all its phases. *But details tell nothing essential about architecture, simply because the object of all good architecture is to create integrated wholes.*

Understanding architecture, therefore, is not the same as being able to determine the style of a building by certain external features. It is not enough to *see* architecture; you must experience it. You must observe how it was designed for a special purpose and how it was attuned to the entire concept and rhythm of a specific era. You must dwell in the rooms, feel how they close about you, observe how you are naturally led from one to the other. You must be aware of the textural effects, discover why just those colors were used, how the choice depended on the orientation of the rooms in relation to windows and the sun. Two apartments, one above the other, with rooms of exactly the same dimensions and with the same openings, can be entirely different simply because of curtains, wallpaper and furniture. You must experience the great difference acoustics make in your conception of space: the way sound acts in an enormous cathedral, with its echoes and long-toned reverberations, as compared to a small paneled room well padded with hangings, rugs and cushions.

Man's relation to implements can be broadly described thus: children begin by playing with blocks, balls and other things which they can grasp in their hands. As time goes on they demand better and better tools. At a certain stage most children have the desire to build some sort of shelter. It may be a real cave dug into a bank, or a primitive hut of rough boards. But often it is no more than a secret nook hidden among bushes, or a tent made with a rug draped over two chairs. This "cave game" can be varied in a thousand ways but common to them all is the enclosing of space for the child's own use. Many animals are also able to create a shelter for themselves, by digging a hole in the ground or building some sort of habitation above it. But the same species always does it in the same way. Man alone forms dwellings which vary according to requirements, climate and cultural pattern. The child's play is continued in the grown-up's creation, and just as man progresses from simple blocks to the most refined implements, he progresses from the cave game to more and more refined methods of enclosing space. Little by little he strives to give form to his entire surroundings.

And this—to bring order and relation into human surroundings—is the task of the architect.

CHAPTER II

Solids and Cavities in Architecture

Seeing demands a certain activity on the part of the spectator. It is not enough passively to let a picture form itself on the retina of the eye. The retina is like a movie screen on which a continuously changing stream of pictures appears but the mind behind the eye is conscious of only very few of them. On the other hand, only a very faint visual impression is necessary for us to think that we have seen a thing; a tiny detail is enough.

A visual process can be described as follows. A man walking along with bent head receives an impression of blue jeans; a mere hint will suffice. He believes that he has seen a man though actually all he saw was the characteristic seam running down the side of the leg. From this one small observation he concludes that a man has passed him on the sidewalk, simply because where there is that sort of seam there must be jeans and where there are moving jeans there must be a man inside them. Usually his observation ends here; there are so many things to keep an eye on in a crowded street that he cannot bother his mind with his fellow pedestrians. But for some reason our man wishes to have a closer look at the person. He observes more details. He was right about the jeans but the wearer is a young girl, not a man. If he is not a very dull person he will now ask himself: "What does she look like?" He will then observe her more closely, adding detail to detail until he gets a more or less correct picture of her. His activity can be compared to that of a portrait painter. First he forms a rough sketch of his subject, a mere suggestion; then elaborates it enough for it to become a girl in jeans; finally he adds more and more details until he has obtained a characteristic portrait of that particular girl. The activity of such a spectator is creative; he *re*creates the phenomena he observes in his effort to form a complete image of what he has seen.

This act of re-creation is common to all observers; it is the activity that is necessary in order to experience the thing seen. But *what* they see, what they re-create when observing the same object, can vary enormously. There is no objectively correct idea of a thing's appearance, only an infinite number of subjective impressions of it. This is true of works of art as of everything else; it is impossible to say, for instance, that such and such a conception of a painting is the true one. Whether it makes an impression on the observer, and what impression it makes, depends not only on the work of art but to a great extent on the observer's susceptibility, his mentality, his education, his entire environment. It also depends on the mood he is in at the moment. The same painting can affect us very differently at different times. Therefore it is always exciting to return to a work of art we have seen before to find out whether we still react to it in the same way.

Usually it is easier to perceive a thing when we know something about it beforehand. We see what is familiar and disregard the rest. That is to say we re-create the observed into something intimate and comprehensible. This act of re-creation is often carried out by our identifying ourselves with the object by imagining ourselves in its stead. In such instances our activity is more like that of an actor getting the feel of a role than of an artist creating a *picture* of something he observes outside himself. When we look at a portrait of someone laughing or smiling we become cheerful ourselves. If, on the other hand, the face is tragic, we feel sad. People looking at pictures have a remarkable ability to enter a role which seems very foreign to them. A weak little man swells with heroism and a zest for life when he sees a Hercules performing daring deeds. Commercial artists and producers of comic strips are aware of this tendency and make use of it in their work. Men's clothes sell more readily when they are displayed on athletic figures. The observer identifies himself with the handsomely built model and believes he will resemble him simply by donning the same apparel. A middle-aged woman uncritically buys the costume she sees in an advertisement on a shapely glamour girl. The boy with glowing cheeks who sits spell-bound over the adventures in a comic strip imagines himself in Tarzan's or Superman's stead.

It is a well known fact that primitive people endow inanimate objects with life. Streams and trees, they believe, are nature spirits that live in communion with them. But even civilized people more or less consciously treat lifeless things as though they were imbued with life.

In classical architecture, for example, we speak of supporting and supported members. Many people, it is true, associate nothing particular with this. But others receive the impression of a heavy burden weighing down the column, just as it would a human being. This is very literally illustrated where the supporting element has been given human form, such as a Caryatid or an Atlas—a petrified giant straining all his muscles under his load. This same conception is expressed in Greek columns by a slight outward curvature of profile, the "entasis," which gives an impression of straining muscles—a surprising thing to find in a rigid and unresponsive pillar of stone.

The various parts of a chair are given the same designations that are applied to human and animal members—legs, arms, seat and back. And often the legs are actually shaped like animal parts, such as lion paws, eagle claws, and doe, goat, ram, or horse hooves. Such surrealistic forms have appeared periodically ever since ancient times. Besides these, there are many examples of "organic" forms which neither resemble nor represent anything found in nature. They were employed in the German Jugend style around the turn of the century and appeared again not only in a later furniture style but also in other design. An automobile, for instance, is called a "Jaguar" and in keeping with the idea association its lines recall the speed and brute force of its namesake.

Even things which in no way suggest organic forms are often invested with human characteristics. We have already seen how riding boots and umbrellas can affect us as real personalities (p. 31). In Dickens' novels, buildings and interiors acquire souls in some demoniacal way corresponding to the souls of the inhabitants. Hans Andersen, who gave a ball and a top the power of speech, used to cut out silhouettes in which a windmill became a human being, just as it was to Don Quixote.

Portal of Palazzetto Zuccari, Rome

Portals are often described as "gaping," and the architect of the Palazzetto Zuccari in Rome actually formed an entrance of that building as the gaping jaws of a giant.

The Danish architect Ivar Bentsen, who throughout his life retained a remarkably original view of architecture, said at the dedication of a new wing of a folk high school in Denmark: "We usually say that a house *lies*, but some houses *stand*—towers always stand. This house here *sits* with its back against a hill, gazing towards the south. Go outdoors in any direction and observe it and you will see how the schoolhouse lifts up its head and peers out over the broad countryside south of the town."

Such animation of a building makes it easier to experience its architecture as a whole rather than as the addition of many separate technological details. To Dickens a street of houses was a drama, a meeting of original characters, each house speaking with a voice of its own. But some streets are so dominated by a conspicuous geometric pattern that even a Dickens cannot give life to them. There exists from his hand a description of the view from the Lion Inn in the old town of Shrewsbury in England: "From the windows I can look all downhill and slantwise at the crookedest black-and-white houses, all of many shapes except straight shapes," he wrote. Anyone who has visited one of the towns in Shropshire with their tarred half-timber Tudor houses will remember the strong impression made by the broad black lines on white ground and will understand that here even Dickens must see shapes and not strange personalities.

But how do we experience a street when we perceive the houses as geometric forms? The German art-historian A. E. Brinck-mann has given an elucidating analysis of a picture of a certain street in the little German town of Nördlingen.

"The beauty of the situation at Schäfflersmarkt in Nördlingen is due entirely to the fine relations of its forms. How then are the proportions of the two-dimensional picture converted into pro-portions in three dimensions, into a conception of depth? The windows are of almost identical size which gives the same scale to all the houses and makes the three-storied in the background outgrow the two-storied in the foreground. All roofs show ap-proximately the same pitch and complete uniformity of material. The ever-diminishing network of the tiles helps the eye to ap-prehend the distances and thereby also the real size of the roofs. The eye passes from smaller to larger roofs until it finally rests on the all-dominating one of the Church of St. George. Nothing indeed creates a more vivid illusion of space than the constant repetition of dimensions familiar to the eye and seen in different depths of the architectural perspective. These are the realities of the architectural composition and their effect is enhanced by the difference in tones caused by the atmosphere. When finally the complete forms of the houses are realized—the two-bayed and the four-bayed, all with horizontal divisions—the tower seems overwhelming in size with its concisely articulated masses rising high into the air."

By keeping an eye on the picture while reading Brinckmann's description it is possible to experience the whole thing exactly as he describes it. But when you see the place in reality you get a very different impression of it. Instead of a street *picture* you get an impression of a whole town and its atmosphere. Nördlingen is a medieval town surrounded by a circular wall. Your first glimpse of it, after passing through the town gate, gives you the conception of a town consisting of identical houses with pointed gables facing the street and dominated by a huge church. And as you penetrate further into the town your first impression is confirmed. Nowhere do you stop and say: "It should be seen from here." The question that interested Brinckmann, how a two-dimensional picture can best give the impression of three dimensions, does not arise. You are now in the middle of the picture itself. This means that you not only see the houses directly in front of you but at the same time, and without actually seeing them, you are aware of those on either side and remember the ones you have already passed. Anyone who has first seen a place in a picture and then visited it knows how different reality is. You sense the atmosphere all around you and are no longer dependent on the angle from which the picture was made. You breathe the air of the place, hear its sounds, notice how they are re-echoed by the unseen houses behind you.

There *are* streets and plazas and parks which were deliberately laid out to be seen from a particular spot. It might be a portal or a terrace. The size and position of everything seen from there were carefully determined to give the best impression of depth, of an interesting vista. This is particularly true of Baroque layouts which so often converge at one point. An interesting example of this, and one of the sights of Rome, is the celebrated "view through the keyhole." On Mount Aventine, above the Tiber, the peaceful Via di Santa Sabina leads you past ancient monasteries

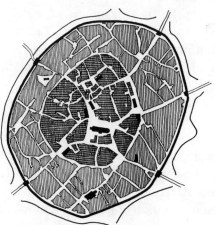

Schäfflersmarkt with St. George's Church, Nördlingen, from Brinckmann
Below, plan of Nördlingen. Scale 1:15000

Views of Nördlingen from the city gate to Schäfflersmarkt
There is no particular spot from which to experience the street

and churches to a small piazza embellished with obelisks and trophies in stucco. Above a brown door to the right are the arms of the Knights of Malta. But the door is closed and barred. Through the keyhole alone you can get a view of the sequestered precincts. And what a view it is! At the end of the deep perspective of a long garden walk you see the distant dome of S. Peter's swelling against the sky.

Here you have all the advantages of a deliberately planned view because you see reality as through a telescope, from a fixed point—and nothing interferes to distract your attention. The view has only one direction and what is behind the observer plays no part in it.

But this is a rare exception. Ordinarily we do not see a *picture* of a thing but receive an impression of the thing itself, of the entire form including the sides we cannot see, and of all the space surrounding it. Just as in the example of the girl in jeans, the impression received is only a general one—usually we do not see any details. Rarely can a person who has "seen" a building give a detailed description of it. If, for example, a tourist visiting Nördlingen suddenly saw the church, he would immediately realize it was a church. We regard a church as a distinct type,

Church of St. George, Nördlingen, seen from Schäfflersmarkt
The impression of the buildings is formed from a series of observations

a symbol as easily recognized as a letter of the alphabet. If we see the letter L we recognize it without knowing what sort of L it is, whether bold-face or lean-face, whether grotesque or Antiqua or any other type. Simply seeing the vertical and horizontal strokes together tells us that it is an L.

In the same way we know that we have seen a church when we have merely received an impression of a tall building combined with a steeple. And if we are not interested in knowing more we usually notice no more. But if we are interested we go further. First we attempt to verify the original impression. Is it really a church? Yes, it must be; the roof is very high and steep and at the front there is a tower like a block standing on end. As we observe the tower it seems to grow. We discover that it is higher than most towers, which means that we must alter our first impression of it. During the visual process we seem to place the octagonal tiers on top of the rectangular block—originally we had not noticed that they were octagonal. In our imagination we see them rising out of the square tower like sections of a telescope until the work of re-creation—which the entire visual process is—ends at the topmost tier where it is checked and terminated by the little rounded calotte. No, it is not finished at that. To complete the picture it is necessary to let the crowning lantern rise out of the skull-cap and add the small flying buttresses and pinnacles at the corners of the square tower.

The mental process that goes on in the mind of a person who observes a building in this way is very much like that which goes on in the mind of an architect when planning a building. After having roughly decided on the main forms he continues by adding details which shoot out from the body like buds and thorns. If he has had manual training in one of the building trades he knows how the individual parts are produced. He mentally prepares the materials and combines them in one large structure. It gives him pleasure to work with the different materials, to see them change from an amorphous mass of ordinary stone and wood into a definite entity, the result of his own efforts.

About 45 miles north of Paris lies the town of Beauvais with its great cathedral. Actually it is only the chancel of a cathedral that was never completed but its dimensions are so enormous that it can be seen for miles, towering above the four-storied houses of the town. The foundations were laid in 1247 and the vaulting was finished in 1272. It was one of those heavenward-aspiring Gothic structures with pillars like tall, slim trees which seem to grow right into the sky. They were about 144 feet high. The construction proved too daring, however, and the vaulting collapsed in 1294. The church was rebuilt about forty years later with the vault just as fantastically high as before but supported now from the outside by flying buttresses. And the builders were apparently so fascinated by this purely structural problem that they made a virtue of necessity and turned the supporting members into a rich composition of piers and arches embellished with sculpture. In other words, purely structural features were treated æsthetically, each one given almost sculptural form.

The architect can become so interested in forming all the structural parts of a building that he loses sight of the fact that construction is, after all, only a means and not an end in itself. The elaborate exterior of Beauvais Cathedral was developed to

Beauvais Cathedral

make possible the fantastically high nave—not from any desire to create a spiked monument striving to pierce the heavens with its sharp points. But it is understandable that the architect can come to the conclusion that the aim of his calling is to give form to the materials he works with. According to his conception, building material is the medium of architecture.

But, you may ask, can there be any other? And the answer is yes; it is possible to have quite a different conception. Instead of letting his imagination work with structural forms, with the *solids* of a building, the architect can work with the empty space —the cavity—between the solids, and consider the forming of that space as the real meaning of architecture.

This can be illustrated by an example. Ordinarily a building is made by assembling the materials on the site and with them erecting a structure which encloses the space of the building. In the case of Beauvais the problem was to raise a church on a flat tract of land. But let us suppose the site to be an enormous, solid rock and the problem to hollow out rooms inside it. Then the architect's job would be to form space by eliminating material— in this case by removing some of the rock. The material itself would not be given form though some of it would be left standing after most had been taken away.

In the first instance it is the stone mass of the cathedral which is the reality; in the second the cavities within the mass.

This can also be illustrated by a two-dimensional example which may make it clearer.

If you paint a black vase on a white ground, you consider all the black as "figure" and all the white as that which it really is— as background which lies behind the figure and stretches out on both sides with no definite form. If we try to fix the figure in our minds we will note that at the bottom the foot spreads out on both sides and above it a number of convexities also project on to the white ground.

But if we consider the white as figure and the black as ground —for example, a hole in the figure opening into a black space—

then we see something quite different. Gone is the vase and in its stead are two faces in profile. Now the white becomes the convexities projecting out onto the black ground and forming nose, lips and chin.

We can shift our perception at will from one to the other, alternately seeing vase and profiles. But each time there must be an absolute change in perception. We cannot see both vase and profiles at the same time.

The strange thing is that we do not conceive the two figures as complementing each other. If you try to draw them you will involuntarily exaggerate the size of the area which at the moment appears as convexities. Ordinarily convex forms are seen as figure, concave as ground. This can be seen on the figure above. The outline here being a wavy line it is possible to see either black or white convexities, as you choose. But other figures, such as one with a scalloped edge, are not perceptually ambiguous.

There are innumerable classic patterns which are identical no matter how you look at them. A good example is found in weavings in which the pattern on the reverse is a negative reproduction of the one on the right side. But most two-dimensional motives that are carried out in two colors force the observer to see one of the colors as figure and the other as ground.

In Carli in India there are a number of cave temples. They were actually created, as I have described above, by eliminating material—that is by forming cavities. Here the cavity is what we perceive while the solid rock surrounding it is the neutral background which was left unshaped. However, here the problem is a more complicated one than in two-dimensional figures. When you stand inside the temple you not only experience the cavity—the great three-aisled temple hollowed out of the rock—but also the columns separating the aisles which are parts of the rock that were not removed.

I purposely use the word "cavity" because I believe it illustrates this type of architecture better than the more neutral word "space" so often used in architectural writing nowadays.

This question of terms is of great importance. German art-historians use the word "Raum" which has the same root as the English "room" but a wider meaning. You can speak of the "Raum" of a church in the sense of the clearly defined space enclosed within the outer walls. In Danish we use the word "rum" which sounds even more like the English word but has the wider meaning of the German Raum. The Germans speak of Raum-Gefühl, meaning the sense or conception of the defined space. In English there is no equivalent. In this book I use the word *space* to express that which in three dimensions corresponds to "background" in two dimensions, and *cavity* for the limited, architecturally formed space. And I maintain that some architects are "structure-minded," others "cavity-minded;" some architectural periods work preferably with solids, others with cavities.

It is possible to plan a building as a composition of cavities alone but in carrying it out the walls will almost inevitably have certain convexities which will intrude on the observer in the same way as the pillars in the Carli temples do. Though we begin by conceiving the temples as compositions of architectural cavities, we end by experiencing the bodies of the columns. The opposite can also happen. You see a house under construction and think of it as an airy skeleton, a structure of innumerable rafters sticking nakedly into the air. But if you return again when the house is finished and enter the building, you experience it in quite a different way. The original wooden skeleton is entirely erased from your memory. You no longer think of the walls as structures but only as screens which limit and enclose the volume

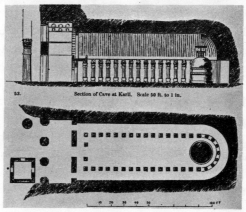

Section of Cave at Karli. Scale 50 ft. to 1 in.

Cave temple at Carli,
India. The temple was
hollowed out of rock
Above:
·view of interior
Below: Section, plan

of the rooms. In other words, you have gone from a conception of solids as the significant factor to a purely spatial conception. And though the architect may think of his building in terms of construction, he never loses sight of his final goal—the rooms he wishes to form.

Gothic architecture was constructional; all bodies were convex with more and more material added to them. If I were to point out a typical example of a Gothic form I would select the sculpture of St. George and the Dragon in Nicolai Church in Stockholm. The sculptor was so enamoured of spiky excrescences of all kinds that no human being could possibly conceive the shape of the space surrounding the dragon.

A column during the same period became a whole cluster of shafts. Seen in cross-section it looks as though it had broken out on all sides in small, round knobs. The transition from Gothic to Renaissance was not only a change from dominating vertical elements to dominating horizontal ones, but above all a complete transformation from an architecture of sharp and pointed structures to an architecture of well-shaped cavities, the same sort of change as that from seeing the vase as figure to seeing the two profiles.

The illustrations in the work of the great Italian architectural theorist, Serlio, clearly show the new conception. A favorite Renaissance form is the circular, domed cavity. And just as the Gothic pillar was expanded on all sides into a cluster of shafts, the Renaissance cavity was enlarged by the addition of niches.

Bramante's plan for S. Peter's in Rome forms the loveliest ornament of round, domed cavities joined together and expanded on all sides by semicircular niches. If you consider the dark, hatched part as "figure" you will find that it forms a very queer remainder after the cavities have been hollowed out of the great wall masses. It is like a regular cave temple dug out of the enormous building block.

The plan, as we know, was changed and the church today has a somewhat different form. The sensitive observer will be dis-

Detail of the group "St. George and the Dragon" in the Nicolai Church, Stockholm
The picture shows the broken lance and dragon's head
Example of typical Gothic forms

appointed at his first sight of the enormous room. In full daylight it seems uncomfortably vast and empty. But during the great church festivals the room is transformed. You now experience

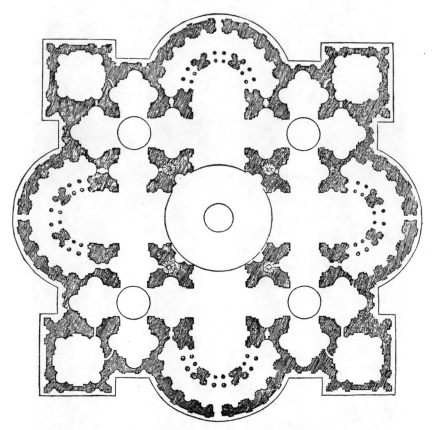

Bramante's plan for St. Peter's, Rome. From Serlio

it as the colossal cave temple of the hatchings. All daylight is shut out and the light of thousands of candles and crystal chandeliers is reflected from the gold of vaults and cupolas. The church is now truly a vast sepulchral temple closing around Saint Peter's grave.

St. Peter's, Rome, in candle light. From a drawing by Louis Jean Desprez, 1782

*Copenhagen City Hall in which the architect has particularly stressed the solids
terminating them in peaks and spires*

*Copenhagen Police Headquarters. Here the architect has formed the cavities
The courtyards seem to be hollowed out of the enormous block*

The extraordinary transition from Gothic love of construction to Renaissance cultivation of cavities can still be experienced. The Danish architect Martin Nyrop (1849–1921), who designed Copenhagen's City Hall, had like so many of his contemporaries the carpenter's view of architecture as a structural art. It might be called a Gothic conception. He was interested in making his constructions an æsthetic experience, among other ways by giving them rich ornamentation. Everywhere he showed how the building was put together. The City Hall is a large edifice with an irregular, spiked silhouette of gables, spires and pinnacles.

By the time the next monumental building was planned for Copenhagen the conception of architecture had swung full round. This building, Police Headquarters, is formed as a huge block cut off flat at the top. Nothing projects above the horizontal band which finishes the walls. All construction is carefully hidden; it is impossible to form any idea of how the building was made. What you experience here is a rich composition of regular cavities: circular and rectangular courts, cylindrical stairways, round and square rooms with absolutely smooth walls. Nyrop's City Hall is embellished with semi-circular bays which push out from the façade. The many cavities of Police Headquarters, on the other hand, are enriched with semi-circular niches pushing back into the solid masses of the walls.

Plan of Minerva Medica, Rome. From Palladio

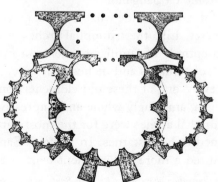

Contrasting Effects of Solids and Cavities

Southeast of S. Peter's in Rome there is a Renaissance monument of unique classical beauty—the city gateway *Porta di Santo Spirito*, by Antonio da Sangallo.

It is rather difficult to decide what it is that gives this structure its noble character. Like the triumphal arches of ancient Rome it is composed entirely of familiar elements: a vaulted archway in a framework of columns and niches. But here, on the slightly curved front, every one of these old elements appears in a new and sublime form, amazingly whole and impressive. The niches in antique triumphal arches were for the most part simply small recesses designed to hold statues. In Porta di Santo Spirito the niche has acquired a more independent existence as a concave

The illustration above shows Porta di Santo Spirito, Rome

form cut deep into the stone mass. It is so large that it breaks through the cornice which forms the impost of the gateway arch; this continues into the niche, casting deep shadows and giving added emphasis to the cylindrical body. Of equal simplicity and greatness are the half-columns with their slightly swelling forms, which are emphasized by the curves at their bases.

The gateway was never finished but you do not feel that anything is lacking. It would hardly be enhanced by the addition of capitals and all the other details usually found on traditional entablatures. The horizontal cutting-off of the columns gives a clear picture of their cylindrical form. The most striking thing about this piece of architecture, however, is that it is without ornament; it has only bold, clear-cut mouldings which outline the main forms at decisive points and emphasize important lines by the dark shadows they cast. The whole thing is done with such power and imagination that the observer feels he is confronted by a great building though in reality it is only a large relief, an embellishment of the wall surrounding an archway. The rhythmic alternation of strikingly concave and convex forms produces an effect of order and harmony. There is a fitting interval between the contrasting shapes so that the eye can get its fill of the one before passing on to the counter-movement of the next.

This was how the elements of classical architecture appeared to the Italian people of the Renaissance. They experienced them in the beautiful Roman ruins which at that time, as still today, were undoubtedly even more impressive than they had been in their original form. Marble facings, bronze and gilded ornaments, sculpture, and all small details, had disappeared. Left standing were only the great main forms, the noble wall masses with their vaults, columns and niches. The Renaissance architectural theorists succeeded in transferring this aspect of sublimity and grandeur to the illustrations in their books on architecture, in which simple woodcuts gave the main structure alone, without any petty details. And in this same spirit Antonio da Sangallo created his Porta di Santo Spirito.

Michelangelo: Porta Pia, Rome

About twenty years later Michelangelo designed for the walls of Rome another gateway of a very different character: the *Porta Pia* at the city's eastern boundary. The spectator who tries to take in every detail of this gateway will feel no sense of harmony or balance. It is impossible to choose any one form and attempt to get a lucid picture of it without having its antithesis force its way into the picture demanding to be noticed. The most bizarre details are crowded together in fantastic combinations: hard against soft; light, projecting bodies set in deep, dark recesses. The broken lines of the square arch are seen together with the large, round relieving arch containing the human mask. In the dark shadows of the triangular pediment motive is piled on motive: tensely coiled volutes, a hanging garland and a large white inscription plate. While in Sangallo's gateway one perfectly formed part follows another across the entire surface, in Michelangelo's an unbelievable number of Baroque details are drawn together from the large flat wall to the center, where they clash in mighty conflict. And holding aloof from it all are the large windows on either side with their simple details of impressive weight and serenity.

Sangallo's gateway represents a striving for balance and harmony. Michelangelo's is deliberately restless, an effort to create an architecture that was felt to be dramatic.

A period of rigorously correct architecture is often followed by one in which the buildings deviate from accepted canons. For the truth is that when once we have become familiar with the rules, the buildings that comply with them become tiresome. Therefore, if an architect wants his building to be a real experience he must employ forms, and combinations of forms, which will not let the spectator off so easily but force him to active observation. We saw on page 47 that it is impossible to see both profiles and vase at the same time and that an act of will is necessary if we want to look from one to the other. In the same way a three-dimensional composition in which the spectator is expected to perceive both convexities and concavities demands an energetic effort on his part, a constant change of conception. Another way to make a strong impression is to employ familiar forms that have been given an eccentric turn which will take the spectator by surprise and force him to regard the work more closely. In both cases it is a question of creating purely visual effects. An architect who is interested in construction for construction's sake, or in cavity for cavity's sake, will not employ such contrasts or mannerisms. It is difficult to imagine anyone trying to emphasize the effect of a large iron bridge by using contrasting detail. But the artist who wishes to create a sensational visual effect can employ such means to accentuate certain parts of the work. He contemplates it, adds something which will emphasize or give relief, steps back, looks at it again and ponders

Porta Pia, Rome. Cornice seen from below

how to obtain a still stronger effect—for instance, by creating a
deep cavity, a black shadow behind the light contours of a body.

At all times there can be found Mannerists of this kind with
a predilection for the visually effective. But there are also entire
periods which are wholly dominated by such æsthetic tendencies.
After the efforts of the Renaissance to create a pure and simple
style which, like its classical prototype, would give perfect balance and harmony, there followed a period in which artists all
over Europe threw themselves into an orgy of mannered experi-
mentation. It came naturally—not as a break with the foregoing
era but as a continuation of it in which the artists worked ex-

clusively with the same forms. In architecture they employed the classical columns, portals, mouldings and cornices that had come down to them; in painting and sculpture they took over entire figures and poses from classical statues instead of studying the life around them. In other words, their problem was to carry on the work that had been started by their predecessors, to arrange rather than create. Effective presentation was therefore of fundamental importance. Earlier centuries had produced tapestries which were veritable meadows of lovely flowers, each one of which had been botanically studied before being planted in the green field. But now magnificent bouquets and luscious fruit arrangements appeared in which the most unlikely flowers and fruits were placed together in combinations that were rich in contrasts of form and color.

Porta Pia,
Rome.
Detail of
side
windows

In architecture this Mannerism could lead to such an over-luxuriant bouquet of forms as Michelangelo's Porta Pia but it could also produce such an exceedingly charming building as the *Palazzo Massimo alle Colonne* in Rome (designed by Baldassare Peruzzi, d. 1536).

Today it stands in a broad street, Corso Vittorio Emanuele, but it has not always done so. The street was widened to its present width in 1876. To understand the conditions for which the building was designed we must imagine ourselves back in the old Rome so excellently presented on Giambattista Nolli's map from the middle of the 18th century (p. 68). On it the house blocks are indicated by the dark hatchings and in between the narrow streets form a weird, light pattern. But not only the streets and squares are shown in white; also entrance courts and church interiors appear as light cavities in the dark mass. Here we find our palace lying in the narrow, curving *Strada della Valle*, at the end of an even narrower street, *Strada del Paradiso*. With its quite small dimensions the building fits perfectly into its surroundings, its lovely convex façade following the curve of the street. At that time it was impossible to stand off from it far enough to see the building in its entirety. From the opposite sidewalk you could command a view of the open loggia of the ground floor, which seemed to form a continuation of the street. Instead of the arched entrance of most Renaissance houses it has a deep, murky cavity cut into the solid block, a cavity that seems even darker behind the light pairs of columns. The entire motive was so unusual that the palazzo was known as Massimi's palace with the columns. From the loggia a stone passageway leads to a little court where the same contrast of cavity and columns is repeated. The two sides of the tiny court are formed by a colon-nade with a barrel vault, again a cavity, which here is pierced by three light openings cutting obliquely into the cylindrical surface of the ceiling. From this court a new stone passageway leads to a smaller court of different character and from there through dark archways to the rear street.

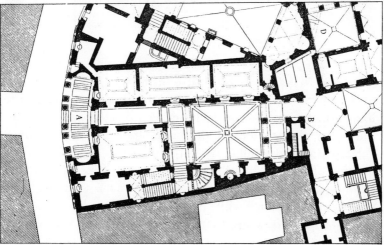

Palazzo Massimo alle Colonne, Rome. Façade. Plan with original layout of streets. Scale 1 : 500

Palazzo Massimo is not bizarre in the way Porta Pia is but it is dramatic in its own fashion. In contrast to other palaces of the Renaissance, which seem to have been created according to a single law that permeates the buildings from start to finish, Palazzo Massimo is full of delightful surprises, a capricious composition of light and dark, open and closed. Like Porta Pia the building seems top heavy. It is in every way a surprising structure to meet in Rome while it would seem entirely natural if the façade had been designed to front a Venetian canal. Your carriage cannot drive into the courtyard but only up to the house, as gondolas are anchored at the steps which lead from the canal to

Palazzo Massimo alle Colonne, in Rome. View of courtyard

loggias and courtyards. It would be wrong to believe that the outer circumstances dictated the unusual design of the building. The architect found certain possibilities in the site and knew how to make use of them. Others saw the result and later many buildings appeared in Rome in which the architects had taken advantage of the spatial effects that are so striking in a city with very narrow streets.

West of the long Piazza Navona is an extremely tangled net of old, narrow streets which are full of surprises: here a little market place teeming with colorful life, there a medieval tower, now a dark palace of the Early Renaissance, again, a Baroque

church dominating its little entrance court. The word "corridor" has often been used in connection with these narrow Roman streets and here, at any rate, there is one street which is narrower than many a Roman palace corridor, and much murkier. Towards its far end it narrows even more, terminating in a dark, covered passageway, which leads to the forecourt of the church of S. Maria della Pace.

Rome has many squares which are the forecourts of churches but this one is undoubtedly one of the most unusual, closed in as it is by architectural structures on all sides. The church itself is much older, but the entrance court and church façade were designed and built as one composition by Pietro da Cortona about 1660. Though the buildings which form the walls of the entrance court have different functions, he was permitted to give them uniform façades. They are decorated in thè same crisp style which a hundred years earlier had been employed on the exterior of the Palazzo Massimo. Tuscan pilasters are pressed in between

North entrance to Santa Maria della Pace, Rome. Point A on plan, page 69

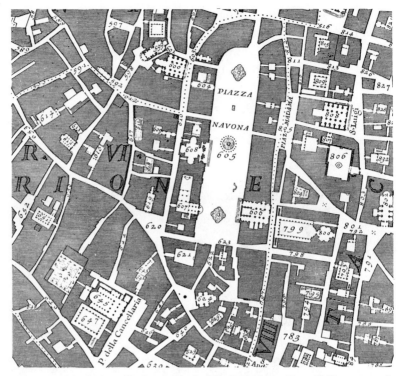

Plan of neighborhood surrounding S. Maria della Pace, Rome. From Nolli's map, 1748. Above left, no. 599 marks Church of S. Maria della Pace; opposite it, no. 600, Church of S. Maria dell' Anima; below, no. 625, Palazzo Massimo

slabs of stucco. It might be called drawing-board architecture. The stucco slabs are by no means meant to give the illusion of heavy masonry but only to suggest, in low relief, a pattern of well-known motives. These modest, somewhat theatrical façades are like a huge folding screen bent at many angles around the church. They make it impossible to stand off at any distance and view it but this fact only makes the grandeur of the architecture more effective. The lower part of the church has the same horizontal elements as the other buildings on the court but in higher relief. Like the Palazzo Massimo the façade opens to a loggia with columns, and they are almost the same columns even to their

S. Maria della Pace, Rome. Pietro da Cortona's façade seen from point B on plan below

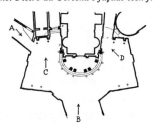

Detail of S. Maria della Pace, Rome, seen from point C on plan p. 69

dimensions. But here instead of a slightly convex front we have a boldly curved portico which pushes well out into the little court. It is a breath-taking experience to come from the dark, narrow passage out to the sunlit courtyard and then turn and see the church entrance like a little round temple surrounding a cool, shadow-filled cavity. And as you gaze upwards the extraordinary arrangement of the reduplicated columns is even more dramatic.

The upper part of the façade is a composition of curved and angular forms. The interior seems to be pressing against the wall, pushing it out in a tremendous bulge. You can almost see how it bursts apart, forming an opening which is held together by the

segmented pediment which fills the shadow of the large gable.
And this whole huge, tense body emerges from the deep niche
of the concave façade, just as the loggia below juts out into the
court. When, as here, architecture is interpreted as forms which
swell, press, push out, etc.—all motion phenomena—it is really
an attempt to show how the spectator re-creates the building
masses through the visual process. The observer is given a great
deal to think about, though nothing that can tell him what the
building itself contains. It is pure external drama, a play of
architectural forms. The little entrance court has become a stage.

Detail of S. Maria della Pace, Rome, seen from point D on plan p. 69

*Façade of
S. Carlino
in Rome.
Church and
monastery
designed by
Borromini*

*Detail of
entrance to
S. Carlino
monastery
in Rome*

Campanile of S. Andrea delle Fratte in Rome. Architect: Borromini

But dramatic it certainly is, a splendid example of how forms alone can give an impression of great magnificence. This was what the Counter Reformation needed and therefore Rome was embellished by many church façades in which swelling forms set in deep recesses were employed with great virtuosity.

This is true of entire façades such as S. Agnese, S. Andrea on the Quirinal, and S. Ivo. But it is also true of many details. Next to the church of S. Carlino alle Quattro Fontane, by Borromini, with its spectacular concave-convex façade, is the doorway of the small cloister attached to the church. It is framed in a moulding like the petrified folds of a drapery, in which a deep groove is surrounded by heavy beads and these round forms are set against angular ones. Borromini, who created this edifice, also designed the campanile of S. Andrea delle Fratte. No Mannerist artist would have any reason to be ashamed of this fantastic work.

From Frank Lloyd Wright's "Falling Water," Bear Run, Pennsylvania. The waterfall out over which the building projects

The most remarkable of the many squares in Rome is undoubtedly the one containing the Fontana di Trevi. Here, the narrow streets converge into a lower, oblong piazza surrounded by yellow ochre buildings. The ground has been hollowed out to receive an enormous stone basin which is filled with water. And in violent contrast to this purely spatial composition the fountain's architect has piled up a landscape of rugged rock which clashes with the smooth-hewn stone of the basin. Water pours in cascades over the rocks and in the foam smooth marble Tritons pull up their fiery white steeds, while above it all a Renaissance palace, with columns, statues and heavy cornices, presides serenely over the fantastic scene.

In Pennsylvania, in our day, Frank Lloyd Wright has created his fantasy over cavity, rock, architecture and sculpture. It is not in a city environment but in a mountain valley far out in the

Frank Lloyd Wright's "Falling Water," showing contrast between the very rustic stone and smooth white concrete walls. Note how the house has been fitted into the natural surroundings

country. You approach it through a lovely wood where the sun barely penetrates the thick foliage of the trees, wandering along narrow, winding paths until quite suddenly you see the light, horizontal lines of the house in among the vertical trunks and leafy boughs of the trees. In an often reproduced photograph the building appears as a composition of large concrete slabs cantilevered out over a waterfall, high up against the sky. In reality, however, it is much less forced. When the leaves are on the trees you cannot see the house at all in the distorted perspective. The visitor finds it an intimate and friendly dwelling, an organic part of its environment of valley slopes and natural scenery. The waterfall rises where layers of rock jut out into the light of the deep ravine, forming a great platform which breaks the fall of the water as it streams down from a higher level to a lower. Wright has continued Nature's composition of horizontal ele-

Frank Lloyd Wright's "Falling Water." The smooth forms of the sculptured figure are placed in juxtaposition to the rusticated blocks of stone just as in Fontana Trevi

ments and massive rocks in the green hollow of the valley. The house is composed entirely of horizontal masses that seem as natural there as the jutting rocks of the waterfall, and the occupants live in rooms that jut out over the rushing water. From their windows and balconies they gaze into the crowns of the trees. The building materials are partly rough-hewn stone of a very characteristic rustication and partly smooth slabs of white concrete, with windows of glass and steel. The large living room has a stone floor, part of it the very rock on which the house is built, and walls of glass and stone. With its fine furniture, textiles and works of art, and with its view of the tree-tops, it is a delightfully livable room, marked by quality and culture.

This house is a good example of Frank Lloyd Wright's endeavors to bring architecture into harmony with Nature. When he builds among rocks his houses rise into the air, when he builds

*Frank Lloyd Wright:
Interior of Johnson
Wax Company's
building in Racine,
Wisconsin*

on a plain they spread out horizontally. And he emphasizes the horizontal so that you cannot fail to experience it, for example by means of overhanging eaves that cast long, horizontal shadows.

In his desire to obtain unusual effects he creates a Mannerism of his own with accentuations, recesses, skilful contrasts between concave and convex forms, juxtaposition of raw and refined materials. Just as the house over the waterfall has traits in common with Fontana Trevi, many of his other buildings have Baroque traits. He often produces an impression of extra weight and volume by letting solid bodies penetrate into architectural space. He also works with contrasting forms, curves which change from concave to convex, as in interiors in the famous Johnson Wax building in Racine, illustrated above. In dwelling houses he prefers the so-called "open plan" in which, as in many Baroque compositions, the rooms merge into each other and are articulated and made interesting by the interpenetration of heavy architectural bodies. There is not the same demand today for grandeur and richness in architecture that there was during the counter-reformation. Nevertheless, there have been a number of architects in the past fifty years who have worked with effective contrasts of solids and voids. *Eric Mendelsohn,* in the twenties, gave the publisher's building, Mossehaus in Berlin, an exterior which was just as extravagant as Baroque church façades. But instead of the reduplication of columns, pilasters and other vertical elements, he emphasized all the horizontal ones.

Eric Mendelsohn: Mossehaus, Berlin

In Denmark during the period 1910–20 the architect Carl Petersen attempted to work out a more deliberate doctrine of architectural æsthetics than the previous generation of architects had known. It was materialized in his museum building in the small provincial town of Faaborg. The exterior is a play on the same effects that were used by Baroque architects in Rome: contrasts of concave and convex. The building-line swings back in a great curve to form a small forecourt. This is penetrated by the main wing which projects its mass into the concavity. In this large body there is a cavity—the deep-cut hole of the entrance, and in this the architect has placed the round bodies of columns.

Carl Petersen also formulated his new æsthetics in words—in a lecture with the significant title: "Contrasts." He had great influence on his contemporaries culminating in the mannerist New-Classic style of the Copenhagen Police Headquarters. Palladio was studied but the result was more akin to Peruzzi's Palazzo Massimi. Police Headquarters is a composition of regular cavities joined together in dramatic sequence leading to the innermost rectangular court where the huge stone cylinders of columns are set up in effective contrast. Here, too, in an enormous niche stands a Mannerist statue—the Serpent Killer by Utzon Frank—a contrast both in material and size to the other elements of the court. Likewise, the portals to the murky side-passageways, with ashlar slabs like drawers drawn out from the flat walls, were designed only to create strong visual effects.

Police Headquarters, Copenhagen, view of rectangular courtyard seen from the circular one
Compare p. 63 Palazzo Massimo, Rome

As one walks through the monumental courts of Police Headquarters nothing indicates that they have any other function than
the purely æsthetic one of creating effective contrasts to each
other. The only impression one receives is of a temple dedicated
to "grand architecture," or rather to grand architectural effects.

The employment of masses and cavities together in effective
contrasts leads to works which lie in one of the peripheries of
architecture, close to the art of the theater and at times to that
of sculpture. But still they belong under architecture. There are
problems which are best solved by utilizing visual effects and
there are architects who do their best work in dramatic architecture of this kind. Indeed, there are even entire periods which
find their true expression in it.

Police Headquarters, Copenhagen. Passageway in rectangular courtyard

CHAPTER IV

Architecture Experienced as Color Planes

We do not perceive everything as either mass or void. Very distant objects often seem completely flat. Many cloud formations are seen only as two-dimensional figures against the background of the sky. A distant stretch of coast coming into view across water appears merely as a silhouette. You see the outlines but have no impression of depth. Even Manhattan, with its depth of thirteen miles, looks like the painted back-drop of a theater when seen across the water from the deck of an in-going ship.

There is one place in the world where such phenomena—so often observed near the water—are very striking, and that is Venice.

Coming from the Adriatic, which forms a dramatic seascape of wave crests with shadows of an amazingly intense ultramarine, to the flat waters of the lagoons behind the string of islands, you feel that you have been transported to an unreal world where the usual concepts of shape and form have lost their meaning. Sky and water merge into a brilliant blue sphere in the middle of which dark fishing boats glide and the low islands appear simply as floating horizontal stripes.

Venice itself looms like a mirage, a dream city in the ether. And this impression of unreality persists even to the very threshold. The colored phantoms of the buildings, floating on a watery surface, seem to be lighter than all other houses one has ever seen. In bygone days Venice must have looked even more exotic. At that time, when every self-respecting town was surrounded by the most menacing and impenetrable fortifications, the first impression of this metropolis must have been of a sort of earthly paradise where fear was unknown, with houses with delicate and graceful arcades swarming with carefree people. Large, lively market places opened out towards the sea. Where other cities

North side of
S. Mark's
Square,
Venice,
decorated
with rugs.
May 1956

fortified a mountain top with thick walls without a single opening, Venice was built right out into the shallow waters with
brightly painted palaces completely pierced by windows and
columned loggias. Instead of emphasizing weight and solidity,
Venice allured with gaiety and movement.

Here the Orient began, but a transfigured, an idealized Orient.
The city was a veritable treasure house with its wealth of colorful
merchandise from three continents. And when it decked itself in
festive array no other European city could rival its magnificence.
From the Orient Venice had learned how to transform her houses
and create an atmosphere of splendor by hanging costly rugs
from her windows. Still today during the great festivals you can see
the buildings surrounding S. Mark's Square adorned in this
fashion. Even without such ornament the buildings are extraordinary monuments of a unique city culture. The entire north

Corner of Palazzo Danieli, Venice. Note window which is more like an exterior decoration—a hanging prayer rug with brackets like heavy weights on each side— than like a hole in a wall

side, the Procuratie Vecchie, is a gallery-like building five hundred feet long, from about the year 1500. On the street level is an arcade with shops and above are two stories with windows between columns, like boxes in a theater. When rugs are hung from the closely spaced windows they completely cover the many carved details of the façade. Instead of a richly sculptured block the building is transformed into a collection of figured color planes. After having seen this decoration you feel that you understand many of the other buildings better. They are attempts to make this festive array permanent. The mosaic floors in S. Mark's, you discover, are really costly carpets fashioned of colored stones, and the pattern of the marble facing on the ancient brick walls of the church resembles fine rugs with broad colored borders.

But most remarkable is the Doges' Palace. Contrary to all architectural rules its walls are massive above and completely

Doge Palace, Venice. The large, heavy upper part appears light because it is faced with
rose-colored and white marble in a large, checkered pattern

pierced below. But this is not at all disturbing; there is no feeling
of top-heaviness. The upper part, though actually solid and
heavy, seems light, more buoyant than inert. This effect was
achieved by facing the walls with white and red marble in a large
checkered pattern. The design is cut off arbitrarily at the edges as
if the whole thing were a huge piece of material that had been
cut to fit. In artificial light the façade, standing luminous against
the dark sky, becomes completely unearthly; but even in glaring
sunlight it is no stone Colossus on feet of clay but a gay, tent-like
surface. At the corners are twisted columns and they too are
different from other columns. They are so thin that they no
longer are supporting elements but simply edgings, like the cord
upholsterers use to hide seams.

*Venetian palace with façade which resembles a set-piece of Oriental rugs:
prayer rugs and others with decorative borders and corded edgings*

Potemkin is said to have erected scenery which conjured up
flourishing towns along the route of a journey made by Catherine
the Great. One imagines that he got flimsy frames covered with
painted canvas to give the effect of solid buildings. In Venice
the very opposite was done. Along the Canal Grande one great
palazzo lies beside the other. They are deeper than they are wide,
built entirely of stone and brick faced with marble or stucco in
shades of Venetian red or burnt sienna. And the architects have
succeeded in making them look like colorful *fiesta* decorations of
unsubstantial materials.

The Canale Grande is above all a place of festivity, the scene
of magnificent regattas. For centuries the canal dwellers have
taken pleasure in decorating their houses with flowers, banners,

and costly rugs, as they do on S. Mark's Square—and here too attempts have been made to make the decoration permanent. These light palaces are not, like other buildings, characterized by certain architectural elements that are supporting and others that are supported. They are simply divided by narrow mouldings, twisted like cords or decorated like borders, and between the mouldings are stretched the color planes of the façades. Even the windows seem to be surface ornaments rather than openings in walls. Pointed arch openings are inscribed in a rectangular field so that they look like Islamic prayer rugs hung on the façade, those rugs which themselves are flat representations of a niche in a wall. There are also real Gothic buildings in Venice, churches of daring construction. But the Gothic of the palaces is merely ornamental. The pointed arch embellished with Islamic tracery is simply a decoration on the surface of the façade. In Gentile Bellini's painting one of the buildings (still to be seen in Venice) seems to be entirely hung with rugs. The wall surface has a textile pattern, the windows resemble prayer rugs and between two of them still another rug seems to be hung, while the whole is edged with cords and borders. Also the Venetian buildings of the early Renaissance, with their flat facings of many-colored marble, often give the impression of light structures in festive array. The buildings of the two periods are the same, it is only the exterior pattern that has changed: the pointed arch has been replaced by the round one.

There seems to be a connection between the colorfulness of Venetian architecture and the special light that prevails in Venice where there are so many reflections from the southern sky and the water. Shadows never become black and meaningless; they are lighted up by shimmering, glittering reflections which give the colors a special richness. During the period when architecture was light and colorful, Venetian art too glowed with intense color, as still can be seen in S. Mark's. We can only faintly imagine how well it suited the Doges' Palace when its interior was decorated with the pure color tones of medieval flat painting.

Detail of Gentile Bellini's painting of the Miracle at Rio di S. Lorenzo

Canal Grande Venice, seen from the steps of Palazzo Grimani. To the left the base of the Renaissance palace, a heavy block in contrast to the lighter palaces in the background

But the late Renaissance brought new architectural ideals to the airy city. Buildings were no longer to depend on color planes for effects but on relief, on massiveness and dramatic shadows. In our time a Venetian façade commission prevented the erection of a house designed by Frank Lloyd Wright on the ground that it did not harmonize with the general character of the city. In reality Wright's mannerism is no more alien to the old Venetian architecture than the late Renaissance was. It was when those great, massive buildings with heavy rusticated masonry and boldly projecting orders were introduced among the lighter structures with their colorful walls that the decisive break in the orderly evolution of Venetian architecture occurred.

The interior of the Doges' Palace was gutted by fire in 1483 and later the enormous rooms were decorated according to the taste of a new era. The building, outwardly so light in color and

material, was now given the heaviest of interiors. The walls were
covered with grandiose paintings which, with their perspectives
and violent shadow effects, disrupt all planes. The ceilings were
stuccoed in high relief and given so much ornament, so much
color and gilt, so many paintings creating the illusion of great
depth, that you actually feel crushed under the weight of it all.

The Venetian buildings teach us something of how an appearance of either weight or lightness can be created in architecture. We have already seen that markedly convex forms give an
impression of mass while concave ones lead to an impression of
space. In Venice we learn that buildings can be formed so that the
only impression they give is of planes.

If you make a box of some heavy material, such as thick,
coarse-grained planks dovetailed together so that the thickness
of the wood is obvious at every corner, the weight and solidity of
the box will be immediately apparent. The buildings of the late
Renaissance were like such boxes. The heavy quoins gave the
illusion of exaggeratedly thick walls. By employing such devices
Palladio designed buildings with brick walls that looked as though
they were made of the heaviest ashlar.

But just as a building can be made to appear heavier than it
actually is, it can also be made to appear lighter than it is. If all
irregularities on the wooden box were planed away and all crev-
ices filled out so that the sides were absolutely flat and smooth,
and it was then painted a light color, it would be impossible to
tell what material it was made of. Or if, instead of paint, it were
covered with a figured paper or textile it would seem to be very
light, as light as the material covering it. This is what was done
with the Doges' Palace and with many other buildings in Venice.

During the late Renaissance and the following periods a building which appeared light was not considered real architecture.
Lightness was all right for tents and other temporary structures
but a house should be solid and look solid; otherwise it was not a
house. And if an edifice was to be grander than its neighbors it
was made so by added weight and added ornament.

The French Revolution did away with Baroque ideals. Wigs went out of fashion. During the following decades several attempts were made to produce lighter, less cumbersome architecture. French Empire, English Regency and German Biedermeyer created buildings completely covered with smooth stucco painted in pale colors; all very light and graceful compared to Baroque architecture. But this phase lasted only a short time and heaviness and ornament returned once more.

It was not until this century that architects the world over concentrated their efforts on the creation of a weightless architecture.

An illuminating example of this is a villa built in 1930 in a pine forest outside Berlin. It was lighter and more open than anyone hitherto had imagined the house of a wealthy man could be. The owner, a Berlin banker, was proud of his new house and eager to show it to people. "Nowadays burglary is the order of the day in Germany," he said. "I have a house in Berlin which is much more solidly built and full of antiques and works of art. But in such a house you go in constant fear of burglars. Therefore I've rented it to a man who is not afraid to take the risk and built this house for myself instead. Out here, as you can see, I have no treasures. I have only what is necessary for a comfortable and independent life. The entire west side of the living room is one long glass wall which can be shoved aside when the sun shines and closed when it is cold, so I can always sit in here and enjoy nature outdoors. If thieves should come they will be able to see everything there is from outside, and over-all carpeting and a few pieces of bright steel furniture are no temptation to house-breakers."

Here was a new attitude towards life which found expression in the light architecture of cubism. Many different conditions had led to this result. As to the form itself, the architects had borrowed it from painting. During the decade before the first world war a school of painting had arisen which, instead of creating an illusion of solids and voids, worked with contrasting color planes. Quite by chance these theoretical experiments came

Luckhardt Brothers: Villa built for Herr Kluge, Am Rupenhorn, Berlin, 1931

to play an important role during the war. Artists who were serving in a French battery at the end of 1914 began painting their position in order to conceal it from the enemy. Earlier, artists would have tried to make it resemble a part of nature but these men chose to hide it under a bizarre, abstract painting. This aroused the interest of a French commander with the result that a "section de camouflage" was formed early in 1915. Two years later the British navy went in for something they called "dazzle painting." With the help of black, white and blue paint laid on in abstract figures the great gray battleships were transformed so thoroughly that it was impossible to tell bow from stern or make out contours or shapes. The heavy hulls became light and airy in their new harlequin dress. Incidentally, it is remarkable to see how strongly this painting—seemingly laid on quite at random—was determined by the artistic idiom of the day. This becomes apparent when it is compared with the camouflage painting of the second world war. Where before the colors had been bright they were now muddy, and instead of the straight lines and triangles of the early camouflage there were now sinuous outlines and undulating shapes.

For most people the cubist camouflage was a demonstration of visual effects they had never seen before. But by the time the war was over everybody was familiar with them and new experiments with cubist forms were made in architecture as well as other arts. One of these was the German film, "Dr. Caligari's Cabinet," made in 1919, in which the action takes place inside the brain of a lunatic where all forms are disintegrated into crooked triangles and other weird shapes. Buildings too were constructed with bizarre lines and shapes. But all these strange forms were only transitional phenomena which left no permanent traces, while attempts to break up the unity of the façade into rectangular color planes proved to be of lasting effect. Compared to the dogged experiments of the Germans to create a new style during the years following the war, Le Corbusier's work in the second half of the nineteen-twenties was of amazing simplicity and clarity. At that time he not only designed buildings but also painted cubist pictures and wrote inspiring books on architecture. In his writings he described how rational everything should be; the dwelling, he said, should be a machine to live in. But the houses he designed were quite different—an attempt to create a cubist framework for everyday life. They were color compositions without weight, just as intangible as the camouflaged ships.

Speaking of a housing project he was designing for the town of Pessac, near Bordeaux, he said: "I want to do something poetic." And he succeeded. These houses represented the utmost that can be done to give an illusion of absolutely weightless elements. If, instead of covering the smooth box we contemplated above with cloth, we were to paint its sides in different colors which met at the corners so that a light gray, for example, bordered on a sky-blue, and there was nowhere the slightest hint

Le Corbusier: Houses in Pessac near Bordeaux. Sitting in a garden on the roof of one of the houses, in the shade of a leafy maple tree, I could see how the sun dappled the Havana-brown wall with blobs of light. The only purpose of the wall was to frame the view. The buildings opposite could be perceived as houses only with great difficulty. The one to the left was simply a light-green plane without cornice or gutter. An oblong hole was cut out of the plane exactly like the one I was looking through. Behind and to the right of the green house were row-houses with coffee-brown façades and cream-colored sides and behind them rose the tops of blue "sky-scrapers"

of structural thickness, then we would see nothing but several color planes without volume. The mass and weight of the box will have disappeared as if by magic.

This is what Le Corbusier did with his houses in Pessac. In 1926 they could be experienced as one huge color composition.

Le Corbusier liked to set his houses on slim pillars so that they seemed to float on air. What you see are not supported and supporting elements, and you feel that the architectural principles that apply must be entirely different from those of traditional heavy architecture. The construction, too, is different.

Le Corbusier used reinforced concrete for buildings in which the floors were supported by a few pillars standing inside the building instead of along the building-line. The outer walls rested on the cast concrete floors. They were meant only as a protective curtain and therefore it was in keeping with the facts when they appeared to be merely thin screens. The windows formed long bands just as they do on the promenade decks of great liners.

The housing estate in Pessac was the most consistent attempt to divest architecture of its mass, but not the only one. Other architects also designed buildings which did away with the old conception of solids and voids. Mies van der Rohe's buildings (Tugendhat in Brno 1930, exhibition building in Berlin 1931) are interesting examples. They have the same simplicity—one might say the same classical aspect—as Le Corbusier's. Mies van der Rohe also employs simple proportions, exact planes, right angles and rectangular shapes. But while Le Corbusier's buildings were like artistic sketches in color, Ludwig Mies' are carefully worked out to the last detail and composed of the finest materials: plate glass, stainless steel, polished marble, costly textiles, fine leather. His buildings do not eliminate their substance as Le Corbusier's did. They consist of screens between the planes of floor and ceiling, but screens of a conceivable weight and thickness. Mies van der Rohe is the son of a stone-mason and his work has always borne the stamp of precision, hardness, and finish. He does not work with cavities, there is no distinct separa-

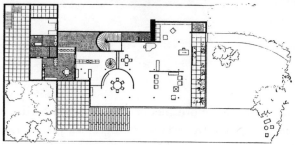

Ludwig Mies van der Rohe: Haus Tugendhat in Brno. 1930

tion between exterior and interior, and the only completely enclosed room is the bathroom. It is a world of screens which may
give a certain background for a group of furniture but can never
create a closed and intimate interior.

Mies van der Rohe's architecture is cold and crisp. The light-
reflecting materials multiply the geometrical forms. There is
in the tendency something corresponding to the architectural
fantasies of the early Renaissance. Their creators also shunned
the closed room where peace and quiet could be found, producing instead unending vistas of rooms opening into each

*From Am Kurfurstendamm,
Berlin 1931.
Kopp & Joseph's perfume shop has
been given a new façade of glass and
chromium-plate. The glass showcases
on the wall inside the shop continue
out through the glass façade and tempt
passers-by with elegant bottles
gleaming in the sun*

other. But there are more modern ideas behind Mies van der Rohe's art. It is akin to certain photographs, just as Le Corbusier's work is reminiscent of cubist paintings. They are the art photographs formed as a sort of collage of several negatives depicting a confusion of semi-transparent buildings merging into each other in a highly incredible fashion.

The architect could now solve many modern problems in an elegant manner—for example, exhibitions. This was true not only of the temporary fairyland of great expositions but also of the ordinary shop-front which requires fascinating materials and the apparent elimination of the barrier between inside and out in order to attract the passer-by. During these years the way of living also underwent a change from the pompous to the unpretentious, though very few went the whole length and lived like the Berlin banker in his functionalistic villa.

Kopp & Joseph's perfume shop in Berlin, 1931, illuminated at night

The new style which in Europe was considered the last word in modernity resembled in many ways that which was traditional in Japan. There they have a pictorial art without perspective or shadows, a line and color art with strange, weightless figures. The Japanese has difficulty in thinking in terms of perspective and when he puts houses in his pictures they become a system of abstract lines. This also characterizes his real architecture.

It is not that he has gotten heavy walls to *look* thin, as in Venetian houses. The walls *are* thin. He forms his houses of screens: paper walls mounted on frames between wooden posts built up over a simple square grid. Many of the screens can be slid aside, transforming the interiors. They do not enclose rooms but form light frames around the inhabitants and their few possessions, flattering openings out towards Nature. The idea of a house built upon a firm substructure is unknown. Japanese houses stand on the ground like furniture in a garden. They have wooden legs which raise the matting-covered floors above the soil. With their verandas, sliding walls, and grass mats they are more like finely made furniture than what we mean by houses.

This architecture of the Far East may be considered as at a more primitive stage than our own. The European learned something during the Renaissance which the Japanese has never grasped. Broadly speaking we can say that his imagination is two-dimensional where ours has three dimensions. But within its limits Japanese art has reached the highest state of refinement. It has a message for us because it employs the very qualities that we have tried to bring out in modern western culture. The entire mode of life and the philosophy of the Japanese have something of the emancipation that we are striving for.

No one has interpreted the Japanese pattern of life better than Lafcadio Hearn, the Anglo-American writer who chose Japan as his second fatherland. In a volume of essays entitled *Kokoro* (1896) he has described "The Genius of Japanese Civilization." The characteristic thing about the culture of Japan, he says, is the extraordinary mobility of the Japanese in every sense of the word. The white man is always seeking stability. His house must be constructed to endure. He makes himself dependent on all sorts of worldly goods. But in Japan everything is in motion. The land itself is a land of impermanence. Rivers, coastlines, plains, and valleys are constantly changing. The average Japanese is not bound to any definite spot. "Ability to live without furniture, without impedimenta, with the least possible amount of neat clothing," says Hearn, "shows more than the advantage held by this Japanese race in the struggle of life; it shows also the real character of some weaknesses in our own civilization. It forces reflection upon the useless multiplicity of our daily wants. We must have meat and bread and butter; glass windows and fire; hats, white shirts, and woolen underwear; boots and shoes; trunks, bags, and boxes; bedsteads, mattresses, sheets, and blan-

A view of the interior of the house Charles Eames built for himself in Venice near Santa Monica, California

kets: all of which a Japanese can do without, and is really better off without. Think for a moment how important an article of Occidental attire is the single costly item of white shirts! Yet even the linen shirt, the so-called 'badge of a gentleman,' is in itself a useless garment. It gives neither warmth nor comfort. It represents in our fashions the survival of something once a luxurious class distinction, but to-day meaningless and useless as the buttons sewn on the outside of coat-sleeves."

Thus sixty years ago Hearn described the Japanese and his way of life as opposed to the white man's. It is interesting to note how much closer we have approached each other since that time. The starched white shirt is no longer a common article of dress simply because we have become much more mobile than we were. We have given up many other superfluous things and in return have come to appreciate nature much more, to have a greater desire to make it part of our daily lives. This is apparent in our houses and their design. Today there are many American dwellings—especially on the west coast—which in materials and planning resemble Japanese houses more closely than they do European. They are light wooden structures elegantly designed on the "open plan," that is to say the rooms are not clearly separated from each other or from the garden.

When Le Corbusier designed his houses in the nineteen-twenties there were many people who could see nothing in them. They saw that something had been built but were not able to perceive it as an articulated form. They expected architecture to form either masses or cavities and as they saw neither one nor the other in his buildings and as, furthermore, he had said that a dwelling should be a machine to live in, they concluded that his houses had no æsthetic form but only solved certain technical problems. Thus it was that people were not able to *see* the most artistic experiment in architecture during that decade. Le Corbusier's work was particularly interesting because it gave a vivid example of a third possibility. If we look once more at the two-dimensional figure that can be seen as either a vase or two profiles, we shall discover that a third conception is possible, that is the line which forms the boundary between black and white. You can trace it, just as you can trace the coast-line of an island, in and out. In other words, it is unsubstantial like a mathematical line. If you try to copy it you will particularly observe all changes in direction and more than likely exaggerate them.

When ordinary people try to draw plans for a house the partitions are usually represented by a single line which indicates the limit of the room or the outside wall. This is the way Le Corbusier's buildings were conceived—not in volume but in mathematically designed planes which formed the boundary lines of certain volumes. And it was the boundaries that interested him, not the volume. He drew attention to the planes by giving them color and cutting them off sharply. The Japanese have a similar conception of architecture though not quite so categori-

cal. In their houses you experience innumerable planes but also 103
wooden posts, which are highly substantial, having structure,
mass and weight. Le Corbusier himself later abandoned the
style he created at the close of the twenties. While at that
time it was abstract painting which inspired him, today his
buildings are more like monumental sculpture. But his early work
had an emancipating effect on other architects. Through it they
discovered that there were other paths to follow than those tradi-
tionally trod. It was incompatible with Le Corbusier's restless
nature that he should create the rational architecture of colored
elements which he had envisioned. But others have taken up the
problem.

When Hertfordshire, England, after the second world war,
was faced with the task of erecting a large number of new schools
without employing the materials and man-power so urgently
required for housing, the problem was solved by a well planned
building program of pre-fabricated units. The first reaction to
these non-traditional buildings was a feeling that they were not
"real" architecture because they seemed so light. Since then the
English people have learned to appreciate them, not only as good
technical solutions but as a new development in architecture.

Today architecture has a wealth of methods to choose from
and the architect can also solve those problems which are best
and most naturally answered by buildings composed of light
planes.

CHAPTER V

Scale and Proportion

Legend has it that one day when Pythagoras passed a smithy he heard the clang of three hammers and found the sound pleasing. He went in to investigate and discovered that the lengths of the three hammer-heads were related to each other in the ratio of 6:4:3. The largest produced the keynote; the pitch of the shorter was a fifth and that of the shortest an octave above it. This led him to experiment with tautly stretched strings of different lengths and he ascertained that when the lengths were related to each other in the ratios of small numbers the strings produced harmonious sounds.

This is only a legend and in my opinion it is too good to be true. But it tells us something essential about harmony and how it is produced.

The Greeks tried to find some explanation for the phenomena they observed. They said something like this: It makes the soul happy to work with clear mathematical ratios and therefore the tones produced by strings of simple proportions affect our ears with delight.

The truth is, however, that a person listening to music has no idea of the lengths of the strings that produce it. They have to be seen and measured. But whatever the Greeks' reasoning, they found that there was some relation between simple mathematical proportions in the visual world and consonance in the audible. As long as no one was able to explain what happens when a tone is produced and how it affects the listener, the relationship continued to be a mystery. But it was obvious that man was in possession of a special intuition which made it possible for him to perceive simple mathematical proportions in the physical world. This could be demonstrated as regards music and it was believed that it must be true of *visible* dimensions also.

Architecture, which often employs simple dimensions, was then as well as later frequently compared with music. It has been called frozen music. That scale and proportion play a very important role in architecture is unquestionable. But there are no visual proportions which have the same spontaneous effect on us as those which we ordinarily call harmonies and disharmonies in music.

The tones of music differ from other, more accidental noises by being sounds produced by regular periodic vibrations and having fixed pitch. Vibrations which result from striking a chord constitute a keynote with a definite rate of frequency and a series of overtones with frequency rates that are double, triple, etc., the keynote rate. Tones with simple frequency ratios have the same overtones and when they are sounded simultaneously a new, absolutely regular period of vibrations will result and it will still be heard as a musical tone. But if sound waves of slightly different periods of vibration are set in motion the sound produced is incoherent and often directly unpleasant. If two sound waves with a frequency ratio of 15:16 arise simultaneously, they will reinforce each other every time the one has vibrated fifteen and the other sixteen times. This will produce extra large oscillations and between these strong blasts there will be points where the vibrations annihilate each other so that they become practically inaudible. The result will be a tone of a weird, quavering, uneven sequence which can be very unpleasant. A sensitive listener may actually get a stomachache from hearing such discords. But there is nothing analogous to this in the visual world, for while we are immediately aware of false tones, small irregularities in architecture can be discovered only by careful measuring. If two strings with lengths in the relation of 15:16 are struck simultaneously the resulting sound will be distinctly unpleasant. But if in a building that is divided in regular bays a difference in proportions of this same ratio were introduced probably no one would notice it. The truth is that all comparison of architectural proportions with musical consonances can only be regarded as metaphor. Nevertheless innumerable attempts have been made to work out principles of architectural proportioning analogous to the mathematical principles of musical scales.

There is one proportion (incidentally without parallel in music) which has attracted great attention ever since the days of antiquity. This is the so-called golden section. Pythagoras and

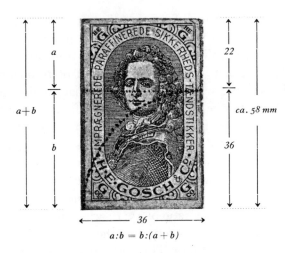

$$a:b = b:(a+b)$$

his disciples were interested in it, theorists of the Renaissance took it up again, and in our day Le Corbusier has based his principle of proportion, "Le Modulor," on it. A line segment is said to be divided according to the golden section when it is composed of two unequal parts of which the first is to the second as the second is to the whole. If we call the two parts a and b, respectively, then the ratio of a to b is equal to the ratio of b to $a+b$. This may sound somewhat complicated but is easily grasped when seen in diagram.

Until recently an ordinary Danish match box, bearing a picture of Admiral Tordenskjold, measured 36 × 58 mm. If we subtract the shorter side from the longer we get $58 - 36 = 22$. It is approximately true that 22 is to 36 as 36 is to 58. In other words, the mutual relation of the sides is that of the golden section.

Unfortunately for Denmark the economic situation of the coun- try made it necessary to reduce the length of matchsticks and therefore Tordenskjold's portrait is now placed in a rectangle, which is regarded as less æsthetic. Formerly the various sizes of paper were also often based on the golden section and the same was true of letter-press printing.

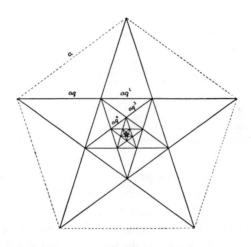

To Pythagoras the pentagram was a mystical and holy symbol. A pentagram is a five-pointed star which is formed by length- ening the sides of a pentagon both ways to their points of inter- section. The relation between the length of one of the sides of a pentagram's point and the side of a pentagon is the same as the golden section. By connecting the five points of the pentagram a new pentagon is formed, from that again a new pentagram, etc. In this way you get an infinite series of line segments which grow according to the rule of the golden section. This çan be drawn in a diagram but these lengths cannot be expressed as rational numbers. On the other hand, it is possible to draw up a series of integers, the ratios of which come close to that of the golden section. These are 1, 2, 3, 5, 8, 13, 21, 34, 55, etc., each new unit being formed by adding together the two immediately preceding. The remarkable thing about this series is that the higher it goes, the closer it approaches the golden section ratio. Thus, the ratio 2:3 is far from it, 3:5 is closer, and 5:8 almost there. Incidentally, 5:8 is the approximation in rational numbers most often used.

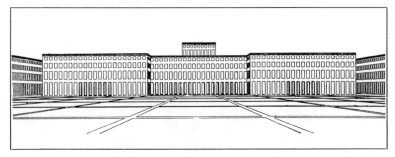

Ivar Bentsen: Project for a philharmonic building in Copenhagen. 1918

Around 1920 many attempts were made in Scandinavia to get away from the romantic tendencies in architecture of the previous generation and to formulate clear æsthetic principles. In Norway Frederick Macody Lund published his great work "Ad Quadratum" in which he sought to prove that the great historical works of architecture were based on the proportions of the golden section. He suggested therefore that those proportions should be used in the reconstruction of Trondhjem Cathedral. In Denmark the architect Ivar Bentsen designed a large project for a philharmonic building in which the proportions were based on the above-mentioned series. It was to be built on a square grid in plan and in elevation to be proportioned according to the golden section rule. The distance between the balusters on the flat roof was the smallest unit, or module. The width of the pillars was set at three of these units and the window width at five. The top row of windows were square, that is 5 × 5, the next below 8 × 5, then 13 × 5, and finally the bottom row (which actually comprised two stories—a ground floor of shops and a mezzanine) was to be 21 × 5.

Even when this has been explained, as here, you cannot experience the interrelationship in the proportions of the philharmonic building in the same way that you experience it in certain
natural phenomena in which there is a rhythmic progression in
proportions. Many snail shells, for example, have whorls which
grow steadily larger in regular progression from the innermost
to the outermost, and this is immediately perceptible. But the
whorls grow in several dimensions so that they continue to have
the same proportions. The windows in Ivar Bentsen's building,
on the other hand, increase only in one dimension and therefore
change successively from square to more than four times as high
as they are broad.

An American author, Colin Rowe, has compared a Palladio villa
with one of Le Corbusier's houses and shown that there is a
remarkable similarity in their proportioning. It is an interesting
study because, besides the buildings themselves, we have both
the plans and the artists' own reflections on architecture.

Palladio's villa, Foscari, lies in Malcontenta on the mainland,
near Venice, and was built for a Venetian about 1560. By that
time Palladio had been to Rome where he had studied the great
ruins of antiquity and he now saw it as his mission to create
architecture that was just as sublime in composition and simple
in proportions. From the architectural world of pure harmonies
one should be able to experience Nature in all its phases.

The main story of the Villa Foscari is raised high above the
ground over a basement which resembles a broad, low pedestal.
From the garden, staircases on either side lead up to the free-
standing portico of the main floor. From here you enter the main
room of the villa, a great barrel-vaulted hall, cruciform in plan,
which runs through the entire building, affording a view of the
garden at the back and of the approach with its large, symmetrically arranged avenues at the front. On either side of this central
hall lie three absolutely symmetrical lesser rooms. This was in
keeping with the Venetian custom of grouping the bedrooms and
living rooms round a large, airy hall in the central axis. But in-

Palladio: Villa Foscari, Malcontenta near Venice. Main entrance façade. The façade design reflects the interior disposition in which a large barrel-vaulted central hall rises to the height of the pediment. The pediment in front corresponds to the loggia on the garden façade shown on the opposite page

stead of the Venetian loggia, which is pushed back into the block of the building, Palladio grafted a classic temple front onto the façade of the villa. Behind it, the house appears solid and monumental. Above the basement the outer walls present a pattern of large blocks in dimensions corresponding to the thickness of the walls—both outer and inner. Within the house, too, you are aware of the thickness of the walls that separate the rooms, each of which has been given definitive and precise form. At either end of the cross-arm of the central hall is a square room measuring 16 × 16 feet. It lies between a larger and a smaller rectangular room, the one 12 × 16, the other 16 × 24 feet, or twice as large. The smaller has its longer wall, the larger its shorter, in common with the square room. Palladio placed great emphasis on these simple ratios: 3:4, 4:4, 4:6, which are those found in

Palladio: Villa Foscari, Malcontenta. Garden front with loggia with enormous columns standing out from the body of the building

musical harmony. The width of the central hall is also based on sixteen. Its length is less exact because the thickness of the walls must be added to the simple dimensions of the rooms. The special effect of the hall in this firmly interlocked composition is produced by its great height, the barrel-vaulted ceiling towering high above the side rooms into the mezzanine. But, you may ask, does the visitor actually experience these proportions? The answer is yes—not the exact measurements but the fundamental idea behind them. You receive an impression of a noble, firmly integrated composition in which each room presents an ideal form within a greater whole. You also feel that the rooms are related in size. Nothing is trivial—all is great and whole.

In Le Corbusier's house in Garches, built for de Monzie in 1930, the main rooms are also raised above the ground but here

Le Corbusier: Villa in Garches

the outer walls hide the pillars on which it stands. Colin Rowe points out that these pillars form nodal points in a geometric net which is divided in a system very similar to the one that could be drawn of the Villa Foscari's supporting walls. In width the proportions in both cases are 2, 1, 2, 1, 2. But while Palladio used his system to give the rooms fixed and immutable shapes and harmonic interrelation in proportions, Le Corbusier has, if anything, suppressed his supporting elements so that you are not aware of them and have not the slightest feeling of any system in their placement. That which is felt to form the fixed and immutable system in the Garches house is the horizontal planes separating the floors. The location of the vertical partitions is quite incidental and, as already mentioned, the pillars are not noticed at all. Le Corbusier himself has stressed the fact that the house is divided in the ratio 5:8, that is, approximating the golden section, but he has hidden it so well that probably no one who has

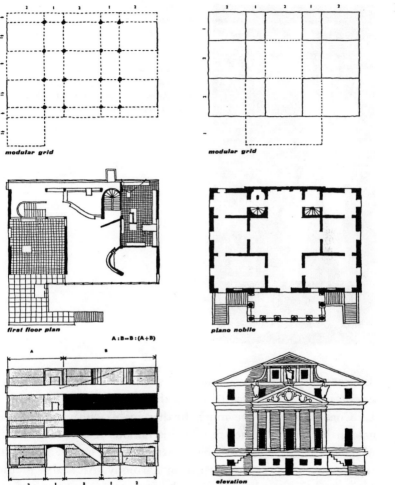

Colin Rowe's comparison of proportions in villas
designed respectively by Le Corbusier and Palladio

seen the building had any inkling of it. There is no similarity in
the principles of composition in the two buildings. Palladio
worked with simple mathematical ratios corresponding to the
harmonic ratios of music and he probably never thought of the
golden section. Le Corbusier worked with rooms of widely

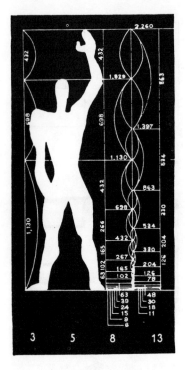

different shapes in an asymmetrical whole and the location of his important divisions was based on the golden section. Since then Le Corbusier has gone much further in his cultivation of the golden section. On the front of his famous residential unit in Marseille he has placed a bas-relief of a male figure. This man represents, he says, the essence of harmony. All scales in the entire building are derived from the figure, which not only gives the proportions of the human body but a number of smaller measurements based on the golden section.

How he has arrived at these results makes interesting reading. You feel that antiquity with its combination of religious mysticism and artistic intuition lives on in this man who, for many people, stands as the representative of rational clarity and modern thought. Originally Le Corbusier placed the average man's

Leonardo da Vinci's ideal man. The man's navel marks the center. With hands outstretched he can reach the circle's periphery

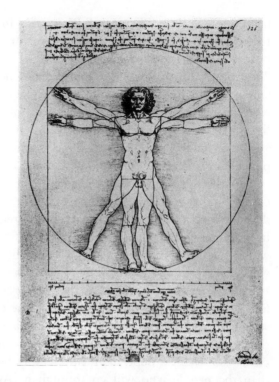

height at 175 cm. This figure he divided according to the golden section rule and got 108 cm. Like Leonardo da Vinci and other Renaissance theorists he found that this corresponds to the height from the floor to man's navel. There was believed to be a deeper meaning in the fact that man, the most perfect creation of Nature, was proportioned according to this noble ratio and that, furthermore, the point of intersection was neatly marked by a little circle. Le Corbusier then divided his navel height in the same way and continued with sub-divisions until he obtained a whole harmonic series of diminishing measurements. He also found—likewise in accordance with the masters of the Renaissance—that man's height with upraised arm was double the navel height, i.e. 216 cm. It must be admitted that this measurement seems of greater importance to the architect than navel height, which it is difficult to find any use for at all in architecture. However, the awkward thing about the raised arm height is that it does not form part of the newly established scale of "beautiful" dimensions. But this did not deter Le Corbusier, who used it as the starting point for a whole new series of golden section measurements. In this way he obtained two sets of figures to work with, which proved to be very fortunate.

But one day he learned that the average height of English policemen was six feet, or about 183 cm, and as average height is increasing the world over, he began to fear that the dimensions of his houses would be too small if he utilized measurements derived from the height of the average Frenchman. Therefore he resolutely established 183 cm as the definitive quantity from which all other measurements were to be derived. He then worked out his two final series of figures which give a great many variations, from very small up to the very largest. What he cannot find in one he is almost sure to find in the other. But still you would seek vainly for a measurement for anything so simple as the height of a door or the length of a bed. Man's height of 183 cm is too small; a door should preferably be somewhat higher than the people who will go through it. And the raised arm height of 226 cm, which Le Corbusier uses as the ceiling height for the smallest rooms in the Marseille block, is too high for a door. In a diagram he has shown how the various measurements, from man's height down, can be employed for different purposes and functions, such as the high desk or platform, table heights, various seat heights, etc. In other words, he has not followed the scientific method of measuring things to determine the extreme limits for their dimensions, but with the help of his two series (in which only man's height and upraised arm height have been determined by measuring) he has arrived at two sets of measurements which he believes in and which therefore *must* suit all purposes. Even if you attached great æsthetic value to the proportions of the golden section it still would not justify the results because the measurements which follow each other in his

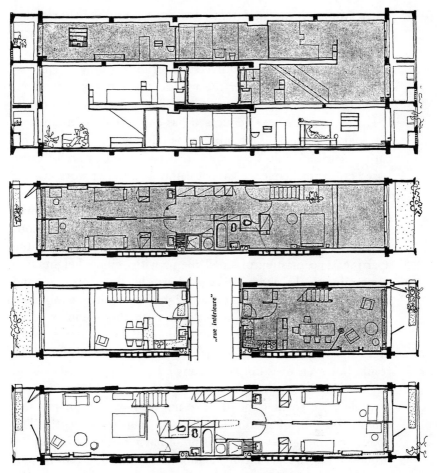

Le Corbusier: The Marseille block. Cross-section and plans of flats. Scale 1:200

tables, and which will often be seen together, have not that ratio
(e.g. man's height and upraised arm height). Le Corbusier himself feels that the two series are of great service to him. As pointed
out earlier, we are not spontaneously aware of simple proportions
in dimensions as we are of harmonic proportions in music. Le
Corbusier, therefore, corrects every one of the measurements that
he arrives at intuitively so that it will correspond to one or the

other Modulor measurement. And as he firmly believes that "Le Modulor" satisfies both the demands of beauty—because it is derived from the golden section—and functional demands. Le Modulor is for him a universal instrument, easy to employ, which can be used all over the world to obtain beauty and rationality in the proportions of everything produced by man.

Let us examine how he himself has employed his Modulor in the Marseille block. This building is entirely different from his earlier works. While they were to be regarded as architecture based on the principles of Cubist painting, his later work is more like gigantic sculpture. The buildings are still raised above the ground but now on enormous substructures. The residential unit in Marseille is like a mammoth box placed on an enormous trestle. The box is divided into innumerable small cells—the apartments, consisting of small rooms with ceiling heights corresponding to the Modulor's raised arm height of 226 cm, and larger living rooms of double that height. The built-in equipment has been dimensioned in accordance with the Modulor rules. Here, the method of proportioning derived from human measurements was to stand the test of practical application. The result, however, does not carry conviction. To keep costs within a reasonable limit the rooms were made as narrow and deep as possible. The smaller rooms have not only extraordinarily low ceilings but are of minimal width and inordinate depth. The depth does not give the impression of having been arrived at by proportioning work. And in relation to it, the large room is not as large as it should be to give a sense of spaciousness in the otherwise cramped conditions.

Nevertheless the building makes a strong impression on the visitor. When you have gone through it, walked about among its gigantic pillars, gone up to the roof and seen the weird landscape of enormous chimneys and other large cast concrete features arranged effectively in relation to the surroundings, ordinary buildings seem strangely petty in comparison. There are several other high apartment buildings in Marseille but not only are they

The colossal underpinning of Le Corbusier's Marseille block, four men high
See also illustrations page 172

slicker in detail, they seem to be composed simply of innumerable small details added together while Le Corbusier's house has real greatness. Why is this so?

Above all, it is due to the fact that the understructure was *not* proportioned according to human measurements—that is in relation to the small apartments—but on a gigantic scale; a fitting substructure for a mammoth box. When you stand down there among these fantastic pillars you are made vividly aware that they were created to support a gigantic building.

Here you find something of the grandeur of Palladio's architecture. In the villa in Malcontenta the old wall decorations still exist and in one of the square rooms the frescoes depict titanic figures in various attitudes. You feel that the house was originally built for such giants and that later ordinary people moved in with their household goods, which seem rather lost in the vaulted stone rooms.

In reality, the ratios of Palladio's villa were derived from the classical columns he used. The columns, taken over from antiquity, were regarded as perfect expressions of beauty and harmony. There were rules for their proportioning down to the smallest details. The basic unit was the diameter of the column and from that were derived the dimensions not only of shaft, base and capital but also of all the details of the entablature above the columns and the distances between them. These ratios were laid down and illustrated in handy pattern-books of the "five orders." Where small columns were used everything was correspondingly small; when the columns were large, everything else was large too. During the early Renaissance buildings were constructed in layers with a new set of columns and entablatures for each story. But Michelangelo and Palladio introduced columns in "large orders" comprising several stories, and from then on there was no limit to how large they could be made or how monumental the buildings. Instead of a small cornice corresponding to the proportions in one story, there now came huge crowning cornices proportioned in relation to the entire building, like the top and bottom parts of Le Corbusier's Marseille block. The pilgrim who came to S. Peter's in Rome must have felt like Gulliver in the land of the giants. Everything was in harmony but adapted to ultralarge columns.

From then on there was an essential difference between the proportioning of monumental architecture and that of domestic buildings. The monumental edifice became even more effective when it was placed in a row of ordinary structures, as Italian churches often were during the Baroque period. The domestic buildings also had their definite rules of proportioning but they were less elastic, not based on column modules but on human dimensions, determined in a purely practical manner.

When we consider how a building is produced we realize that it is fairly necessary to work with standard units. The timber which the carpenter prepares in his lumberyard must fit the brickwork which the mason has built up on the site. The stonecutter's work, which may have been carried out in a distant

Church of San Giorgio Maggiore in Venice, by Palladio
When the colossal columns are seen together with the more normal-sized side-buildings it becomes apparent how immense the church is

quarry, must square with all the rest when it arrives. Windows and doors must be easy to order so that they will exactly fit the openings that have been prepared for them.

The very designation of the most common measuring unit employed in the past—and still used in Great Britain and America—the foot, refers to part of the human body. We also speak of measuring by rule of thumb, the thumb being taken as equal to one inch. A foot can be divided by eye into two, three, four, six, or twelve parts, and these easily gauged divisions are designated by simple numbers in inches. Earlier, there were standard specifications for bricks, timber, distances between beams and rafters in a house, windows and doors—all expressed in simple numbers in feet and inches. And they all fitted together without requiring any further adjustment at the building site. In Denmark half-timber construction particularly had attained a high degree of standardization though it varied in different parts of the country. In some provinces bays were five feet wide, in others six. Each half-timber bay comprised a window, a door, or a section of solid wall. In the stable the width of a bay corresponded to a stall; in the house to the narrowest room—either a pantry or a corridor. Two bays equalled an ordinary room, three the "best room." Heights were also standardized and in some provinces all roofs had the same pitch. In other countries with other methods of construction there were other subdivisions. In England, for instance, they built two-story dwellings for farm-workers in rows, on the beam-ridge principle, with one supporting wall to each house. The subdivision here was in houses—of sixteen feet each—instead of in bays.

In the Baroque period it was not only churches that were built on a monumental scale; palaces too were often given gigantic dimensions. The columns and pilasters of exterior architecture now entered the rooms and dominated them. We are generally told that these palaces were built on such a huge scale to gratify the vanity of princes. Actually, the grandiose dimensions were taken over from classical structures which all architects of that period strove to imitate, and the palaces were neither comfortable nor easy to live in. But with the Rococo period the small room came into its own. Even for official residences the proportioning principles of domestic architecture were employed and in castles and palaces privacy and comfort were now preferred to pageantry and splendor.

Frederik's Hospital in Copenhagen (now Museum of Decorative Art), built by the great Danish architect Nicolai Eigtved about 1750, is a good example of how realistically the architect

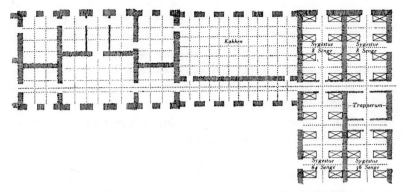

Kaare Klint's proportion study of the rooms in Frederik's Hospital, Copenhagen
To the right, beds measuring 3 × 6 feet and with 6-foot spaces between them

could approach his problem—and of the good result obtained thereby. The entire design, as was only natural, was based on the wards, which were formed as long galleries. Their dimensions were determined by the basic element of a hospital ward: the bed. This was placed at 6 × 3 feet. The beds were to stand with the head-ends against a wall so that it would be possible to approach them from either side and from the foot with one row standing out from the window wall and one from the opposite wall. There was to be six feet between beds in both directions. This gave a room depth of eighteen feet (a bed plus a passage space plus a bed) and a distance of nine feet from bed center to bed center. At every other intervening space a window was placed so that the distance from window center to window center was eighteen feet, i. e. equal to the depth of the room.

In this building, as we see, the dimensions were not determined by columns, or golden sections, or any other "beautiful" proportions, but by the beds which the hospital was built to hold.

This is only one example of the way Eigtved worked. In the course of four years—from 1750 until his death in 1754—he drew up the plans for an entire neighborhood, the Amaliegade district where now the Royal Family lives. He subdivided the ground, made model drawings for individual houses, designed the four Amalienborg Palaces and built Frederik's Hospital. He also made arrangements for all other buildings in the new district so that, when completed, the streets, squares and buildings would form a well integrated composition. This was possible only because he, as the architect who held the whole thing in his grasp, worked with proportions he was entirely familiar with and related them to each other in such a simple manner that he could see it all very clearly in his mind's eye.

Here, comparison of the architect with the composer is completely justified—the composer who must be able to put his composite work into notes by means of which others will be able to perform his music. He can do this because the tones that are available have been firmly established and each note corresponds to a tone with which he is completely familiar.

By a happy accident in the twentieth century Kaare Klint was chosen to restore the hospital building designed by Eigtved in the eighteenth. Earlier, Klint had made exhaustive studies of the dimensions of all sorts of domestic articles as a basis for general architectural proportioning. In his work on the hospital he discovered that when the buildings were measured in meters and centimeters it was impossible to find any coherent system in their proportioning. But measured in feet and inches the whole thing became lucid and simple. In his earlier studies he had found that many of the things we use in daily life were already standardized without our being aware of it. These included bed sheets, table cloths, napkins, plates, glasses, forks, spoons, etc. You can design a new pattern for the handles of spoons but a tablespoonful and a teaspoonful must remain an invariable quantity as long as liquid medicine is given in spoonfuls. Not only were the dimensions standardized but in feet and inches they could be expressed in integral numbers. Many kinds of furniture, too, have standard dimensions based on the proportions of the human body—such as seat heights and the heights of tables for various purposes, etc. Klint was not trying to find a magic formula that would solve all problems; his only desire was to

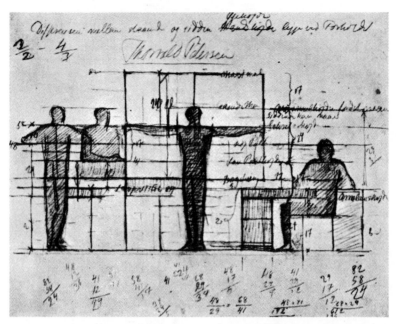

Kaare Klint: Proportion studies for factory-made furniture, 1918

determine, by scientific method, the natural dimensions of architecture and to find out how they could be made to harmonize with each other again—not according to any predetermined ratio but by simple division with nothing left over.

As early as 1918 he designed a whole series of commercial furniture adapted to human measurements and human needs, and until his death in 1954 he continued to improve and supplement it. Today many other designers are working along the same lines. In a world in which mass-production is such a dominating factor it is absolutely necessary to work out standards based on human proportions. But this is nothing new. It is simply the further development of the proportioning rules that were so universally accepted in older days.

In other words, architecture has its own, natural methods of proportioning and it is a mistake to believe that proportions in the visual world can be experienced in the same way as the harmonic proportions of music. For individual objects, such as match boxes, experience has shown that there are certain proportions which appeal to many people for that particular purpose. But this does not mean that there are certain proportions which are the only right ones for architecture. In the Gothic cathedral a breath-taking effect was obtained by bays that were many times higher than they were broad, dimensions which probably no one would find attractive in a single section of wall. But when such abnormally elongated bays are joined together in the right way the result, as shown in the illustration on page 140, may convey an impression of musical harmony to the beholder—not, however, of musical tones but of the regularity which we call rhythm and which we shall investigate in the following chapter.

CHAPTER VI

Rhythm in Architecture

The photograph of the swallows on the wires makes a charming picture with its combination of life and geometry. It is a simple composition of four parallel lines on which a number of birds are perched against a white ground. But within the rigid rectilinear pattern the continuous flashing and fluttering of the birds are variations on a theme which give a completely cinematographic impression of the little flock in vivacious activity. You can almost hear their joyful chirps.

In the world of architecture you can also experience delightful examples of subtle variation within strict regularity. It may be a row of houses in an old street where dwellings of the same type and period were built individually within the framework of a general plan. These houses, too, are variations on a theme within a rectilinear pattern.

It sometimes happens that a sensitive artist deliberately attempts to create effects which in older buildings were entirely spontaneous. The Swedish architect Gunnar Asplund has done so with great artistry in a villa he built in 1917–18 near Stockholm. Le Corbusier, in his church in Ronchamps, sought to give life to wall planes by a pattern of various-sized windows (see page 212). And many other examples can be found, but they are all exceptions.

If a housing block is planned and built as a unit the street will not resemble old streets with rows of houses that were built individually. For while the painter may fill a plane within his composition with continuously changing details, the architect is usually forced to create a regular method of subdivision in his composition on which so many building artisans will have to work together. The simplest method, for both the architect and the artisans, is the absolutely regular repetition of the same elements, for example solid, void, solid, void, just as you count one,

two, one, two. It is a rhythm every one can grasp. Many people
find it entirely too simple to mean anything at all. It says nothing
to them and yet it is a classic example of man's special contribution to orderliness. It represents a regularity and precision found
nowhere in Nature but only in the order man seeks to create.

In the low-lying part of Rome the visitor is immediately struck
by the diversity of the medieval city. It is just as variegated and
just as difficult to find your way about in as a piece of Nature
that has been allowed to grow wild. And if from down there you
go up to the Quirinal, you not only come to brighter and airier
regions but to greater clarity. Ahead of you stretches the long
Quirinal Street in an undeviating straight line. Man has brought
order out of chaos; the hill has been tamed. Along the north side
of the street lies the Quirinal Palace, impressive in its dimensions, its majestic serenity and great simplicity. Its details, too,
are large and simple. The windows are formed as squares or as
two squares, one above the other, and framed in broad, heavy

Fondamenta di Canonica, Venice, with rear of Palace of the Patriarch
Typical Venetian window rhythm

moldings expressively characteristic of the ideals of the period. The distances between windows, both horizontally and verti-cally, are exactly balanced. This continuous repetition is exhilarating rather than tiresome. It is like the opening chords of a great symphony which, in an *andante maestoso*, prepare the ear for complex adventures. The Quirinal is a good starting point for one who wants to experience Rome as an architectural whole.

In the same way the Rue de Rivoli introduces a large scale into Paris. It gives you something to compare the other buildings with. And Rockefeller Center, with *its* great monotony, has given New York a keynote it would otherwise lack.

The rhythm one, two, one, two, will never become obsolete. It has been employed with equal fitness in the rock tombs of Egypt and in Eero Saarinen's buildings for General Motors in Detroit.

Row-houses in Bedford Square, London, from end of the 18th century
Typical London window rhythm

In Venice you find a different window rhythm repeated again and again. It arose because the Venetians like rooms with two windows separated by a broad expanse of wall which thrusts them all the way out to the sides. No one knows what started this custom. Perhaps the wall space was necessary to make room for a fireplace with an outdoor chimney between the windows. At any rate it led to façades with windows coupled together two and two with a narrow pier between. Most people probably imagine that the rooms behind these façades have two windows closely joined, rather than widely separated as they actually are. The coupled windows belong to different rooms.

When a number of one-family houses are built at the same time according to a single plan, the rhythm is often more complicated. The ordinary London terraced house from the eighteenth century has three bays with the entrance door at one side.

There they stand, in waltz measure: one, two, three, one, two, three. Later, around the year 1800, there arose a more complex type with one rhythm for the ground floor and another for the floor above. This is far surpassed, however, by the rhythm of Venetian row-houses. Ever since the Middle Ages the Venetians have built rows of uniform houses for the lower classes. There still exists a row of four-storied, two-family dwellings, built in the fifteenth century, with a different window rhythm at each floor and outdoor chimneys, like the vertical bars of a music score, to keep the rhythm intact. The Calle dei Preti, in which the houses stand, is so narrow that it is impossible to get a good view of the pattern formed by the windows, doors and chimneys from the street itself. But on our measured drawing of the façades it stands forth very clearly; the architect who designed the houses in the fifteenth century must have made a drawing which gave the same picture. As you glance across the front, from left to right, you experience something like a complicated dance rhythm; it could be played on four drums. The architectural details are just as systematically and firmly placed on the façades as the swallows are freely scattered on the four wires; compared to the chirping of the birds, the music here is like the harmony of a fourpart song.

Row-houses from the 15th century in Calle dei Preti near Via Garibaldi in Venice. The façades were probably more uniform originally. Each story had its own rhythm which was repeated with strict regularity across the entire row, the houses being separated by the regularly placed chimneys. Each flat was in two storys, one street-door leading to the dwelling on the lower floors, the other to the one on the two upper floors

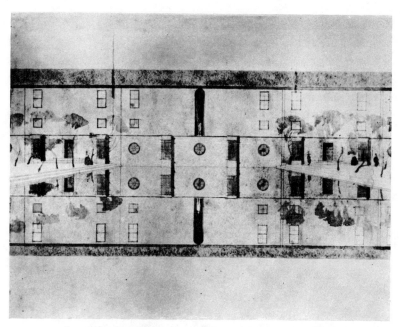

Aage Rafn: Proposal for a courthouse in Kolding, Denmark, 1918
Rafn never had the opportunity to erect a building with such an interesting rhythm

In 1918 the Danish architect Aage Rafn submitted a very unusual design for a court house for a small Danish town—so unusual, indeed, that it was rejected. It had just as exciting a window rhythm as the Venetian houses and a form which—like so many Venetian houses—almost craved mirroring water to give balance. The ground floor had a regular rhythm with alternating round and rectangular windows while the floor above had uniform windows and alternating pier widths. The two rhythms coincided at great intervals.

I am quite sure that most people would notice that all of these façades are rhythmically divided. And yet if you were to ask them what rhythm in architecture means it would be difficult for them to explain, let alone define. The term rhythm is borrowed from other arts involving a time element and based on movement, such as music and dancing.

It is well known that physical work becomes easier to perform when the motions involved are regularly alternated. A job that cannot be done at one stretch is easily accomplished when it is carried out in short, regular spurts so that the muscles have a chance to rest in between. What interests us here is not that the muscles are restored but that the change from one set to the other takes place with such regularity that it is unnecessary to begin all over again each time. The motions are so nicely adjusted that one seems to give rise to the next without conscious effort, like the swinging to and fro of a pendulum. Such regular alternation to lighten work is called rhythm—and by "work," here, I mean every kind of muscular exercise. Dancing for instance is a good example of such work.

There is something mysterious about the stimulating effect of rhythm. You can explain what it is that creates rhythm but you have to experience it yourself to know what it is like. A person listening to music experiences the rhythm as something beyond all reflection, something existing within himself. A man who moves rhythmically starts the motion himself and feels that he controls it. But very shortly the rhythm controls him; he is possessed by it. It carries him along. Rhythmic motion gives a feeling of heightened energy. Often, too, it occupies the performer without any conscious effort on his part so that his mind is free to wander at will—a state very favorable to artistic creation.

Eric Mendelsohn has described how he used to listen to Bach recordings when he had a new project to work on. Bach's rhythms put him in a special state which seemed to shut out the everyday world and at the same time release his creative imagination. Architecture would then come to him in great visions. His sketches show that they were not ordinary, everyday buildings but strange formations that seem to grow and develop rhythmically. During a visit to Frank Lloyd Wright in the twenties he learned that the opposite was true of his American colleague. Wright told him that when he saw architecture which moved him he heard music in his inner ear.

For these two men, then, there is obviously a connection between architecture and music. But it still does not explain what
is meant by rhythm in architecture. Architecture itself has no
time dimension, no movement, and therefore cannot be rhythmic
in the same way as music and dancing are. But to experience architecture demands time; it also demands work—though mental,
not physical, work. The person who hears music or watches dancing does none of the physical work himself but in perceiving the
performance he experiences the rhythm of it as though it were
in his own body. In much the same way you can experience architecture rhythmically—that is, by the process of re-creation
already described. If you feel that a line is rhythmic it means
that by following it with your eyes you have an experience that
can be compared with the experience of rhythmic ice-skating, for
instance. Often the man who forms architecture also works
rhythmically in the creative process itself. This results in a regularity which may be very difficult to express in words but which
is spontaneously felt by those who have the same sense of rhythm.

Rhythmic experience spreads easily from one person to another. A crowd of people who are gathered together to watch
dancing or some sporting event, or to hear music, can be completely absorbed by the same rhythm.

People who live in the same country at the same time often
have the same sense of rhythm. They move in the same way,
they receive pleasure from the same experiences. When we see
the costumes of an earlier age, we often wonder how anyone
could have worn them. At one time those garments were the most
natural thing in the world and now they seem cumbersome and
hampering. This can only be explained by the fact that the people
who wore them moved in a rhythm that was different from ours.
There was intimate connection between the way those people
conducted themselves and the things they wore and used, and it
would take a great deal of coaching before the cleverest actor of
today could give a perfect representation of a person of that period.
In the same way the architecture of various periods must be

looked upon as expressions of changing rhythms. In the Spanish Steps in Rome as depicted by Piranesi we have an illuminating example of this. The architect's problem was a simple one—to create a link between the low-lying Piazza di Spagna and the lofty Piazza della Trinità. The slope was too steep for a ramp; a flight of steps was necessary. Though Rome had many examples of monumental stairways—such as the long, straight flight leading up to Santa Maria in Aracoeli—the new one, when finished, was unique. With its bends and turns, its design seems to have been based on an old-fashioned, very ceremonial dance—the Polonnaise—in which the dancers advance four by four in a straight line and then separate, two going to the right and two to the left; they turn, turn again, curtsy, meet again on the large landing, advance together, separate once more to left and right, and finally meet again at the topmost terrace where they turn to face the view and see Rome lying at their feet. The Spanish Steps were built in the seventeen-twenties when the farthingale was in fashion. Piranesi's engraving gives a faint idea of how the men and women of that day conducted themselves. They knew little about walking but so much the more about the very ceremonious dancing of the period, and therefore they could move gracefully on those steps which so closely resemble the figures of one of their dances—the men in high heeled shoes with toes turned out as they had learned from their fencing masters, the women in tight-laced bodices above their dipping and swaying farthingales. Thus, in the Spanish Steps we can see a petrification of the dancing rhythm of a period of gallantry; it gives us an inkling of something that was, something our generation will never know.

If we believe that the object of architecture is to provide a framework for people's lives, then the rooms in our houses, and the relation between them, must be determined by the way we will live in them and move through them.

In ancient China the emperor was also the chief priest who made the official offerings on which it was believed the welfare of the country depended. This rôle of his was clearly expressed in the

The Spanish Steps, Rome. Detail of an engraving by Piranesi

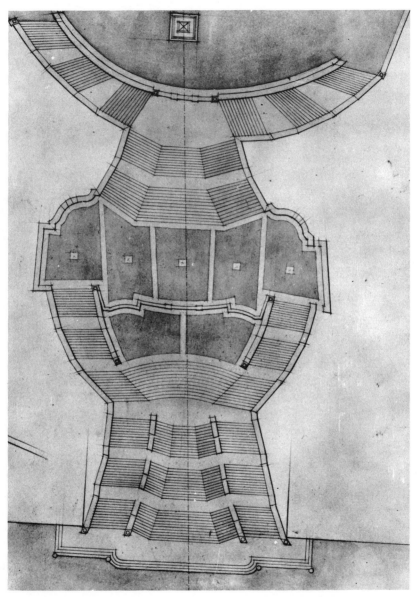

Measured drawing of Spanish Steps in Rome made by students of the Architectural School of the Danish Royal Academy, 1953. Scale 1:500

Peking's central axis formed as a great processional road from palace to temple

plan and entire structure of the capital. Peking was monumentally laid out around a great processional road which led straight through the city from the great throne hall of the imperial palace to the Temple of Heaven. It was an extremely broad road paved with great slabs of stone, and that it was no ordinary highway was clearly indicated. The processions moved on foot, walking along slowly and solemnly. The entire journey was marked by rigid, axial symmetry, from the halls, courtyards and portals of the palace, past symmetrical groups of sculpture and columns, to the monumental temple itself, which is also a composition round a processional axis.

In the same way many sacred buildings of other cults are formed around pageants and rituals in which strict symmetry is observed. In a cathedral the west-east axis, from the main entrance to the altar, is the backbone of the entire building. It indicates the direction of the great religious processions and of the attention of the worshippers. From pillar to pillar, from arch to arch, from vault to vault, the eye follows the great, solemn rhythm throughout the church. When they are seen as part of one continuous movement, it is natural that the individual bays of the building have not harmonic proportions; individually they mean nothing. Like the tones of the organ, they carry on and on and it is only in their rhythmic relation to each other that they obtain meaning. The strange thing about this kind of edifice built as a framework for processions is that even when it is empty the architecture alone produces the effect of a stirring and solemn procession. The churches of the Renaissance have a different rhythm. They are less ecstatic; they do not draw one's attention steadily onward as Gothic churches do. The aim of the Renaissance archi-

Chancel wall in Beauvais Cathedral. The bays are very tall and narrow and cannot be perceived singly but must be experienced as a continuous rhythm

Vaults in S. Giorgio Maggiore church in Venice by Palladio
The building is composed of ideal forms: semi-circular arches and domed vaults

tects was to create harmony and clarity, not tension and mystery. They preferred regular shapes: the square, the octagon, or the circle, covered by a hemispherical vault. Instead of pointed arches they employed semi-circular ones. When the church was not actually a centrally planned building, its rhythm from the west door to the dome of the crossing progressed at a dignified pace from one perfect form to the next. Renaissance architecture was based on mathematical rules of proportioning and, as we have already seen, you intuitively comprehend the harmony which the architect consciously and calculatedly devised.

In Palladio's villas you feel at once that there is proportional relationship in the dimensions of the rooms, which become progressively larger as they approach the great central hall. If into such a firmly integrated composition you introduced new rooms by dividing those already existing, you might obtain several perfectly good extra rooms. But you would feel that they did not belong there. This counter-test proves that Palladio's rooms are rhythmically related in scale and order. But even though his architecture is strictly symmetrical it does not give the impression of having been created for pageantry or ceremonies. Above all, this is due to the dominance and completeness in itself of the central hall. When you are in it you feel no compulsion to move on but are satisfied to contemplate your surroundings from there, to see them in relation to the entire lucid system of directions and proportions. The axis extends into the campagna by means of symmetrically arranged gardens, fields, and avenues of trees, a rhythmic division of the flat countryside, broad and recumbent.

With the culmination of the Baroque a more restless rhythm appeared again. Instead of unity and harmony, architects now strove to create spatial sequences—cavities opening on other cavities. This is seen in Baroque city planning where, instead of single, regular-shaped piazzas, we find stage-like plazas in a variety of shapes, often opening on to each other.

In the same way the monumental architecture of the period was based on dynamic spatial planning with rhythmical series of rooms in which none is treated as an independent unit. This was entirely in keeping with the whole system of Absolutism. The royal residence was formed like an eel trap, that is to say, all movement went in one direction only, each room opening on to another and all leading to a symbol of the regime: a royal statue, a throne room, or an audience chamber presided over by the all-powerful king himself. Though Baroque layouts were not—like Peking—used for processions, they were designed as though they were.

The rhythm employed by one generation in the visual arts and in ornament is often so generally accepted by the following gener-

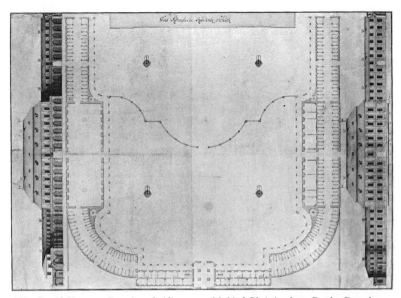

Elias David Häusser: Drawing of riding-ground behind Christiansborg Castle, Copenhagen
Danish National Museum

ation that it is adapted to entire structures. The riding ground
and the surrounding buildings which are part of Christiansborg
Palace in Copenhagen (*c.* 1730) give a splendid example of a
distinctly Baroque rhythm employed in a huge architectural composition. The stables beneath the old court theater form delightful perspectives of vaulted rooms divided by marble columns and
sweeping in a generous curve. But the colonnades along the inner
side of the buildings are even more impressive. They follow a
tense, rhythmic line.

Before 1700, Baroque doors and windows were surrounded by
frames and moldings which seemed to flow in alternating rhythms
from curve to straight line and then, with an abrupt bend, back to
a curve in the opposite direction. The flow was very like the
sharply etched swing of ice-skating. In Christiansborg Palace the
architect transferred this rhythm to an entire colonnade. He undoubtedly enjoyed tracing its movement on his drawing-board.
A skilled designer with a sense of rhythm would be able to draw

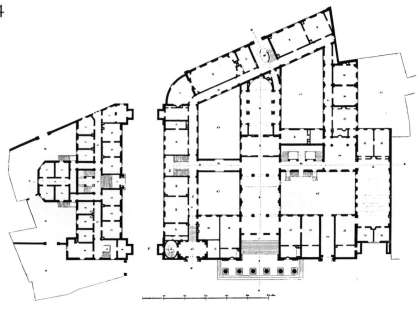

C. F. Hansen: Ground-floor plan of Copenhagen courthouse. Scale 1 : 1000
Note how haphazardly the courtyards are placed in relation to the façade

the two symmetrical lines simultaneously with a pencil in each hand. Starting from the palace at the top of the paper he would begin with a vertical line and continue with a quarter curve in towards the center which he would break off abruptly, just as one does on skates when changing from one foot to the other. Then he would start off again at a right angle, sweep down once more in a straight line, start a new elegant curve in the opposite direction, and then bring it up shortly with a new change of direction at a right angle. On the original drawing—though not in reality—the riding ground is separated from the palace by a wrought-iron fence and that too is designed in great outside-edge curves right across the front.

Though the exteriors of Danish buildings of the Greek Revival, in the early nineteenth century, may resemble Renaissance architecture of the sixteenth century, the buildings themselves seldom possess the rhythmic harmony of Palladio's work. The difference is clearly seen in the city courthouse in Copenhagen. Outwardly the building has the great classical dignity which was Palladio's ideal. But there is no organic connection among the many rooms hidden behind the imposing façade. Each one of them seems to have been planned individually and carefully designed to insure strict symmetry in the disposal of windows and doors. The way they have been put together, however, reminds you of a rather intricate jigsaw puzzle with a great many pieces of all sizes and shapes. Symmetry had become a mere convention. The inflexible rhythm, the measured beat, had spread to buildings where it was anything but natural. But about 1800 people began to realize that something was wrong and architects worked out new forms with a rhythm different from that of official architecture—a rhythm which might be called a 'natural' one. They designed asymmetrical buildings reminiscent of simple country houses seen in Italy and preserved in their sketch books.

Primitive people who move about outdoors with the grace of wild animals—that is to say with beautiful, flowing motions— often have an art that is angular and abrupt. For when a natural rhythm becomes deliberate it has a tendency to stiffen. Archaic art is austere and symmetrical. Thus, the same people may have two different kinds of rhythm: one that is free, the other metrical; one natural, the other ceremonial. A rhythm which is employed by many people at the same time inevitably follows a regular pattern, whether it be the rhythm of a temple ceremony or of military drill. But at a certain cultural level people become conscious of what had hitherto been a natural, flowing rhythm; they discover its grace, study it, imitate it, and deliberately employ it as a form of artistic expression.

On one side of Peking's broad, sacred road—the symmetry axis of the city— lie the imperial pleasure gardens with artistically winding paths following the tortuous curves of artificial lakes over which weeping willows droop their branches. In an old Chinese painting of Peking you get a sort of bird's eye view of courtiers

From Winter Palaces, Peking. Pavilion from which fish are fed

skating on the ice-covered lake of the Winter Palaces. I imagine that earlier in the day these same men had taken part in the great New Year ceremony, walking slowly and solemnly in the Emperor's procession along the broad, straight road to the Temple of Heaven. One portal after the other opened for them until at last they stood before the altar of Heaven. And when the ceremony was over they returned to the Forbidden City, changed to more comfortable attire, and went out on the frozen lake where, as seen in the old painting, they skated about in great spirals.

The Chinese garden was by no means simply an escape from ceremony. It was just as seriously conceived as the symmetrical temple layout; it too was a cult form. In their gardens the Chinese cultivated Nature, just as they celebrated it in their poetry and portrayed it in their art.

Europe also had its landscape garden, partly under the influence of China. In the nineteenth century it took on a definite, stylized form with winding paths. If we did not know better, we might well think it was intended for a carefree, gliding rhythm instead of the sedate movements of our Victorian ancestors. Those meandering paths might have been preliminary studies for the modern motor parkway with its cloverleaf turns and sweeping curves which allow a steady flow of traffic at an even rate of speed. The rhythm in the winding paths of the Victorian garden had probably been mostly enjoyed by the man who drew the curves on paper. But the rhythm of the modern parkway gives daily pleasure and exhilaration to thousands of motorists. It is the intoxicating music of the twentieth century.

If Peking's rhythm was a processional rhythm, a pedestrian rhythm, New York's is a motor rhythm. The city plan of Manhattan, with its broad avenues and numbered cross streets, is just as impressive and simple as that of the old Chinese capital. If you drive at the right speed, for instance along Second Avenue, you can leave street after street behind you as you steadily cross on the green lights. And as the antithesis of the measured beat of that part of town, are the unobstructed motor highways on either side of the city—the East River Drive and the Henry Hudson Parkway. Here are no intersecting streets but only entrance and exit roads which lead the cars on and off the highway in the same flowing rhythm. On and on flows the traffic, across bridges and down broad ramps, farther and farther in sweeping curves out into the country without stop, continuously rising and falling in time with the contours of the earth. This is the New York rhythm, but only at the wheel of an automobile can you mark its beat, feel it in your blood. What a great distance we have come from the polonnaise and minuet dancers of the Spanish Steps! It is not only that we have discarded the old rhythms for others; the ideals of today are entirely different. The rhythm is a new one in practically all fields. The motion picture, which technically consists of innumerable individual pictures, is seen gliding along in uninterrupted flow. The classes which in olden days acquired grace and good carriage through fencing lessons, now play tennis or other ball games. In place of the martial thrust of the fencing foil, carried through in a

Jacopo Tintoretto: Ariadne (sitting) and Bacchus; Venus, her body turning, floats in and takes the star crown off Ariadne's head. Doge Palace, Venice

forward lunge of the stiffly held body, there has come the liberating swing of the tennis racquet in which the entire body turns. But it is probably in swimming that the new rhythm most clearly manifests itself. For centuries swimming, too, bore the stamp of military drill; the breast-stroke was taught to a count of four. In contrast to walking, it was a completely symmetrical form of motion, well suited to soldiers who had to force a river with full marching equipment on their shoulders. And then one day at the beginning of this century someone discovered that the primitive people of the South Sea islands had a much more effective way of swimming—a rolling, uninterrupted, asymmetrical motion—and the *crawl* was introduced in the West. A new rhythm appeared.

This change in the field of sports recalls the change that came in the visual arts with Rafael, Michelangelo, and Tintoretto, a change from a rigid, frontal style to a more plastic one with movement and rhythm. Tintoretto's figures seem to float through space in a weird, gliding manner. In 1951, four hundred years after Tintoretto's painting, the Italian architect Giulio Minoletti, designed a swimming pool with a very similar rhythm.

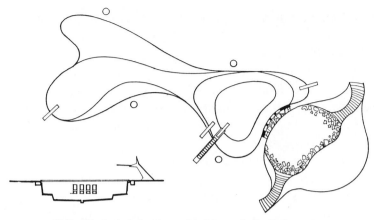

Giulio Minoletti: Swimming-pool in Monza, Italy. Scale 1:1000
From a depression at the sides of the pool you can observe the swimmers through a window as
they swim below the surface where an abstract, mosaic-clad figure is placed

There are buildings which, in their outer form, are reminiscent of ship design, which is based entirely on curved planes. Eric Mendelsohn's Einstein Tower, in Potsdam, anticipated by many years the forms of the streamlined automobile. But just as it is natural and right for ships and fish to be formed so they can move as easily as possible through water, it is unnatural to streamline structures which are not meant to move. The design of buildings, which must be stationary, should be based on the movement that will flow *through* them. But in very few do you find the rhythm of the English garden or the modern motor parkway—naturally enough, in as much as you do not move through a building the way you speed along a motor highway. During the last fifty years, however, the design of many buildings, both large and small, has been based on movements other than the strictly symmetrical ones of earlier times. Innumerable attempts have been made to free architecture from a stiff, ceremonial rhythm.

Frank Lloyd Wright's two homes, Taliesin West and Taliesin East, are good examples of this. The design of both houses is based on the landscape and the way you move through it. In San Francisco he built a glass shop composed around a rising spiral. The rounded and curving forms of the glassware to be exhibited there inspired him to create a room in which everything is rounded and curved instead of rectangular. At the same time he wanted to make passage through the shop more attractive than in the ordinary deep showroom in which you pass rows of shelves straight in line. The curved, rising passageway draws forth the displayed wares so that they are continually seen from new angles and at the same time you get an unobstructed view of the entire shop and all its treasures. The conception is an interesting one but in execution it has become more geometric than rhythmic. It was obviously designed with the help of a pair of calipers and though the forms are all related there is no natural rhythm flowing through them. The same is true of a number of other buildings by Frank Lloyd Wright. He has created many completely symmetrical compositions and others in which he abandoned both symmetry and the

*Frank Lloyd
Wright:
Glass Shop
built for
V. C. Morris,
San Francisco,
1948.
Below, plan.
Scale 1:200*

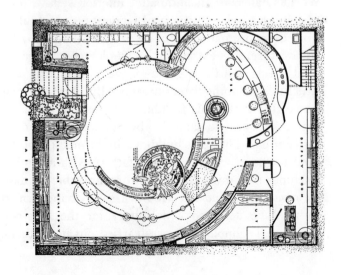

right angle in favor of triangles and hexagons or entirely rounded forms. This can easily become rather forced, a sort of affectation, as in Hannah House in Palo Alto where not only the carport, made to house rectangular automobiles, but also the marriage bed have been formed as rhomboids with angles of 60 and 120 degrees.

Frank Lloyd Wright has opened up new paths and made it possible for other architects to work more freely. However, it is not necessary to abandon rectangular forms, which are so natural and easy to employ; you can easily move freely through rooms that are rectangular and among screens and walls that have lucid and regular forms.

Modern architecture has produced many beautiful examples of buildings with a free rhythm. In Sweden Gunnar Asplund has done much instructive work with interesting rhythms, including both symmetrical and asymmetrical designs for a cemetery in Stockholm. His Stockholm exhibition of 1930 was of particular importance because hitherto so many large exhibitions had misused monumental symmetry. And all his later works are essays in modern rhythms.

There is also a clear and interesting rhythm in all of Alvar Aalto's work. If we compare his Finland building at the New York World's Fair, with its undulating interior wall, with Frank Lloyd Wright's glass shop, I am sure that most people would find Aalto's work the more natural. But he must be judged by his everyday architecture. His extraordinary employment of contrasting textural effects and the organic manner in which he builds up his structures are immediately apparent. But it is his firm grasp of the whole that makes his buildings so amazingly vital. They have something to say to us; he has brought about a union between architecture and life. His buildings are formed round the life to be lived in them, whether it be a factory with assembly lines and machines or a town center with innumerable human functions. He avoids the sterile that is found in so much modern architecture. In 1948 he designed a dormitory for the Massachusetts Institute of Technology. It was carried out in partnership with a

Alvar Aalto:
Transporta-
tion system for
a sawmill in
Varkaus,
Finland

group of American architects and is not in all details as successful
as buildings for which he alone is responsible. But even though a
blemish can be found here and there, it is nevertheless one of the
important monuments of twentieth century architecture. M. I. T.
itself is a large group of monumental buildings with a broad front
towards the Charles River. It should be seen at night when it
lies bathed in floodlights and the heavy limestone walls appear
almost unsubstantial in their ghostly whiteness. From the Boston

side of the river it looks like a fairy palace with its mighty Pantheon dome, its colonnaded front and broad steps. Every night it looms up amidst electric signs and ordinary buildings like a monument of the past, of that August night in 1916 when its picturesque inauguration took place. On the Boston side a procession of Venetian gondoliers led by a doge moved slowly down to the river. After them came other men in long capes with crimson hoods bearing a richly decorated golden casket containing M.I.T.'s charter and other documents. A magnificent gondola carried them over to the Cambridge shore where they again formed a procession and, with measured steps, proceeded along the central axis to the grand colonnaded entrance under the dome.

The entire group of buildings, in stone and bronze and other costly materials, seems to have been created for the sake of that one short pageant alone. It can never be repeated because now the buildings are separated from the river by Memorial Drive, a speedway with its endless stream of motor cars flashing by day and night. And for that matter there is not very much on which to focus such a procession again for the architect neglected to build a hall inside the main building that was worthy of its monumental exterior. In the daytime the façade is lifeless, though this does not mean that there is no life behind it. That life, however, has no connection with the monumentality seen in the floodlights at night. It takes place in quite a different axis. Behind the building is a huge car park where instructors and students leave their cars before entering the building through its main entrance, which is at one end of the building and not in the symmetry axis. There is also a dome here and under it is a long, broad corridor which connects many wings and still more departments. This is M.I.T.'s backbone. Through it pass a steady stream of students in the informal attire of young people: chinos and white shirts—very unlike the ceremonious procession that inaugurated it all in 1916.

It is for these young people that Aalto built his dormitory, Baker House. It too has a long front facing the Charles River. But more in keeping with Cambridge traditions, it is built of red brick.

Massachusetts Institute of Technology, Cambridge, Massachusetts. Aerial photograph

Aalto wanted as many rooms as possible to have a view of the river and therefore he gave the façade an undulating wall. Here is no monumental axis but only a long, unbroken rhythm. This, and the rugged textural character of the building are probably the two things most people notice first. But even more important is the way the entire design is based on the functions of the building, on the life of the students for whom it was built. As in the main building, you enter Baker House from the rear. From the entrance you can go straight through to the dining hall, which projects out towards the river as an independent building with the great undulating wall for a background. From the entrance you can also reach the staircases to the upper floors which crawl up the outside of the building in long, slanting lines, one on each side. They have been compared to a climbing plant which rises from the ground at one spot and spreads out over the walls.

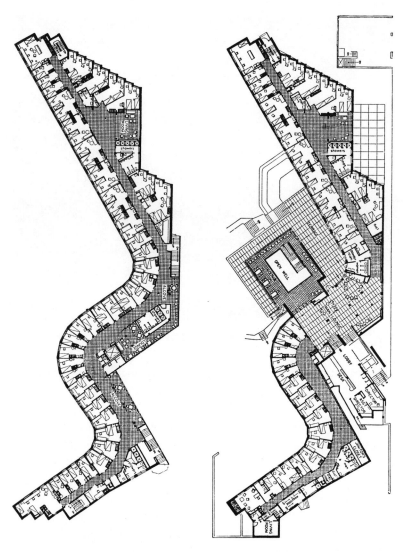

Alvar Aalto: Baker House at M.I.T. Cambridge, Massachusetts
Left: floor plan; right: ground-floor plan. Scale 1:700

Alvar Aalto: Baker House at M.I.T. Cambridge, Massachusetts. Compare p. 183

Much has been said and written about the conformity which is felt to be such a great danger to American youth. It certainly was not conspicuous among the frank and interested students from all over the country who attended M.I.T. while I was there. For these young people Aalto has created a building which entirely avoids the stereotyped rooms and ant-hill atmosphere of old-fashioned dormitories, and the students love it. He has sought to give each one a chance to exist as an individual as well as to lead a corporate life. In Baker House the students can gather in large groups in the lounges on the main floor and in smaller groups in the common rooms on their own floors. Or they can retire to the privacy of their own rooms which, like all parts of the building, are so very human because their design was based on the life that was to be lived in them. Behind the undulating façade the rooms could not be uniform. One has a view up the river, another down;

one lies behind a concave wall, another a convex. Each student feels that his room has a unique location, and each room has been arranged with an eye to the needs and comfort of its inhabitant. There is study space with built-in desk and book shelves near the window and farther back sleeping space with bed and cupboard. And they have all been given character by a happy choice of color and of handsome, robust materials.

The building should be experienced in function. Only by dining with the students in the dining hall, climbing the stairs and visiting them in their rooms will the visitor discover that, just as the church and the palace have their ceremonial rhythms, this large, vital building has its special rhythm, the rhythm of the modern student dormitory.

Alvar Aalto: Baker House at M.I.T. Cambridge, Massachusetts

CHAPTER VII

Textural Effects

On the southern slopes of the Smoky Mountains there is a Cherokee Indian reservation. The houses are hidden in the dense forest
but nearby the highway that runs through the district widens out
in a green valley and here the Indians have set up booths to attract
tourists. Besides the usual refreshment bars and stands selling
gaudy souvenirs and garish picture postcards, there is one booth
which bears witness of an ancient culture, examples of structural
and textural effects that still have something to tell us. This is the
basketwork booth. You can see Indian baskets in shops in many
large cities but they seem much more appropriate here on the
rough wooden shelves of the simple stand built of crude lumber,
with chicken-wire netting for protection instead of plate glass.

Basket weaving is one of the oldest crafts but it is still young and
vital. The Indian baskets on sale in Cherokee, however, are not,
as far as I could learn, products of an uninterrupted tradition.
Interested white people got the Indians to take up their ancient
craft again and to revive the old patterns. But this does not make
the baskets less interesting and they are absolutely worth a closer
study.

Most of the baskets are built up from a square base, with
rounded corners and shapes that narrow towards the circular
opening at the top. The basket-weaving technique itself leads
to certain patterns, just as textile weaving does. It is, of course,
possible to make a serviceable basket without any system in the
weaving at all; but it is more difficult to plait fibers without system
and obtain a good result than it is to follow a definite pattern. The
basketmaker takes pride in making the weaving as even as possible and at the same time clearly showing that there is a pattern.
Though patterns can be very intricate, the technique is so simple
that everyone can appreciate the work. Its very simplicity appeals

to something in us. When two colors are used it is even easier to follow the course of the interwoven fibers around the basket. Patterns can vary from the most elemental to extremely complicated ones, and geometrical designs are particularly suited to the basket-weaving technique. The Indians have realized this and it is amazing to see how exactly their designs work out all the way around. The technique sets a definite limit to the patterns that can be utilized but this very fact seems to have a stimulating effect on the imagination of the Indians. Each new basket they start on becomes a fascinating problem to work out. In all civilizations textile weaving and basketry have led to a wealth of geometric patterns which became so popular that they were transferred to other, less limiting, materials. The technique, too, has influenced other crafts. The earliest clay receptacles were baskets lined with clay to make water-tight vessels.

The Indians had no knowledge of the potter's wheel before Europeans came to America. Their pottery technique was reminiscent of a very primitive form of basketweaving. They first formed the clay into long coils by rolling it back and forth between the palms of their hands. The rolls were then fashioned into rings from which the vessels were built up. Then with their hands the Indians moulded them until the desired shape and a smooth, even surface was obtained. Such pottery is so well formed and evenly rounded that it is difficult to realize it was not made on a potter's wheel.

Certain Indian tribes made not only cooking vessels but entire buildings of clay. The walls of these houses are so smooth that they resemble plastered walls. Originally the entrance was from above, through a hatch in the roof, so that the inhabitants descended into their homes as into a clay vessel. At one side of this

Maria Martinez of San Ildefonso, New Mexico, forming her fine pottery

square house with rounded corners stands a storeroom which is completely round, like an urn. And next to that the family car is usually parked. It too is round and smooth. Here, side by side, we have two illuminating examples of the way man—at very different epochs—has sought to create forms and surfaces which give no impression of structure or origin. The rounded, spray-painted body of the automobile hides a welter of mechanical devices but the car appears as a homogeneous mass made all of one piece. Its polished shell was formed over a solid clay mould which the designer had modeled and smoothed and rounded just as the pueblo Indian, in his day, had smoothed and rounded his clay house.

We continually find the same two tendencies in architecture: on the one hand the rough form of the basket, which emphasizes structure, on the other the smooth form of the clay vessel, which

hides it. Some buildings have stuccoed walls so that you see only the plaster surface; in others the brick is uncovered revealing the regular pattern of the courses. In certain periods the one tendency dominates, in others the other. But there are also buildings in which both are employed together to obtain effective contrasts. The pictures of Frank Lloyd Wright's house, *Falling Water*, on pages 76 and 77 give a good example of this. Its walls of rustic limestone are set against smooth blocks of white cement and shiny glass and steel.

Smooth surfaces must be absolutely homogeneous. It is difficult to explain why minute differences in textural character, barely large enough to be measured by scientific instruments, affect us so strongly. But when we consider that the essential difference between the tones of a fine violin and those of an ordinary one can only be ascertained by the human ear, it is understandable that the sensitive eye can perceive the difference between a firm, noble texture and a rather poor and shoddy one, even when there is no surface pattern and the materials are of the same stuff. You cannot give a reason for your different evaluations but the difference you perceive is real enough. Words can put you on the right track but you have to experience the textural effects yourself to realize what it is all about.

An oft-quoted saying of the Danish sculptor Thorvaldsen is that clay is life, plaster death, and marble resurrection. It is a very graphic remark. You see in your mind's eye three copies of the self-same statue, one in each material, and discover that they are essentially different from each other. Why is plaster so very much less satisfactory than clay? Can it be because we know that plaster is mechanically produced and therefore lacks spirit? Art lovers tell us that old plaster casts have great æsthetic beauty. Thorvaldsen himself was a collector of plaster casts and in the basement of the Thorvaldsen Museum in Copenhagen are many beautiful copies of antique sculpture. But the connoisseur can see a great difference between an old plaster cast and one fresh from the mould. The latter has less character; its surface seems to be less firm. It is like stiffened puffpaste full of pricked bubbles. Furthermore, the fresh plaster not only reflects light but allows some of it to penetrate a little below the surface so that it is difficult to get an exact impression of the form. How very unsatisfactory it can be is best seen by comparing a newly cast statue with an ancient one. The old one seems to have matured. Time has filled up most of the minute pores and the dust of centuries has covered the entire figure with a waxy film so that light can no longer penetrate. Such an old plaster cast is at its best when much handling has worn it smooth and given it an ivory-like surface.

Gray cement castings have even less character than plaster ones. Is there anything more depressing to behold than a cement foundry yard with its display of small couchant lions, Renaissance balusters and poorly articulated mouldings? When they are combined with materials that have more character, such as brick or

stone, the result can be fatal. This is seen time and again in small
but pretentious suburban villas where red brick walls are pro-
fusely decorated with cement details. And we have already seen
how poorly cement and granite combine in the sidewalks of the
Danish capital.

Even the noblest materials lose their character when employed
without skill and understanding. Smooth bronze surfaces are not
satisfactory until they have been refined by the chaser's tools.

In older architecture the only pre-cast ornament employed was
of iron and it was always painted. But in the eighteenth century
English architects began using details of plaster on façades instead
of stone. They were much cheaper and could be ordered from
catalogues containing all the classical items: keystones with Zeus
heads, profiled springers, cornices, mouldings, and entire figures.
At first the castings were apparently mere imitations of real stone
but soon the taste became more refined and the moulded details
were given a light coat of paint. During the first half of the nineteenth century the entire façade of many London houses was
painted a light color; walls, stone and plaster ornament, woodwork, wrought iron details, and even tin gutters, all presented the
same textural effect. (In Denmark architects often have so much
respect for stone that it is allowed to remain in its natural state in
the midst of a painted façade. The effect is very often as unpleasant
as a dirty hand on a snowy white tablecloth—a coarse, work-
roughened hand, at that.) In Regent Street in London it was
stipulated in the leases that all façades must be painted. They
were to be washed once a year and repainted every fourth year.
It was expensive but how elegant it was!

Later, towards the end of the century, these smooth, colorful
façades were regarded as essentially dishonest. Paint on the exterior of a house was as reprehensible as paint on a lady's face. The
architects of the late Victorian era were unable to see how charming it could be. Their feeling about textures was basically a moral
one; only "honest" materials were permissible. Æsthetically, this
meant that they were more interested in rough structures than in

smoothly polished surfaces. They pointed to historical buildings which owed their splendor to robust textural effects though they could just as easily have found famous historical examples with smooth, painted façades. The object of painting a surface is first and foremost to protect it and to make it pleasant to touch. To the Chinese and Japanese, lacquer is not simply a coating that hides the material beneath it but is itself an independent material. They apply the lacquer, rub it down, apply a new coat, and rub it down again. Often there are so many hard layers that it is possible to carve decorations in it. And not only are small objects treated in this way but whole pieces of furniture and even entire buildings. The wooden columns and eaves of Chinese temples, the innumerable brackets under its curved roof, are first given a coating of plant fiber and clay, like thin plaster, and over this the lacquer is applied. Here, there is no question of honesty or dishonesty but only of giving the woodwork a protective covering and brilliant ritual color.

Every boat owner knows that if his boat is not painted regularly it will rot. And in towns where seafarers live you often find that the houses are kept as neatly tarred and painted as ships. This is true of Dutch towns (but not of Venice where the boats, too, are often badly neglected.) In Holland they not only tar the base and paint the woodwork of their houses but often give the entire wall —whether brick or stone—a protective coating too. They stylize the natural colors: brick is painted maroon, base and sills bluish-gray, sandstone cream-color. Besides these there are often gilt and heraldic colors on coats of arms and cartouches. But finest of all are the green doors. No better painting is found anywhere in the world. Though richly detailed and composed of many pieces of wood, these doors are so evenly painted that they appear to be all of one piece. There is not the faintest sign of a brush stroke, not the slightest inaccuracy, but simply a hard, glossy surface that is one with the form. The paint makes the entire house texturally homogeneous though built of many materials, each with its own color.

Painted houses in Middelfart, Denmark

The same glistening neatness is found in many small Danish seaside towns. Even the graceless structures of the eighties and nineties, with walls of machine-made brick and ugly detail, become spruce and attractive after a visit from the painter.

In the London of the nineteenth century, besides the painted stucco houses there were others with naked brick walls which were almost black from soot and smoke and even, at times, a superfluous coating of lampblack. These blackened walls formed an effective background for the light details of painted stone. Here again there was no question of *imitation* but only of obtaining an elegant *textural effect* by combining smooth and rough elements. Though the details were of stone, the æsthetic effect was very

Doorway in Bedford Square, London. Black painted walls with white joints; stone castings around doorway; area wall, mouldings and reveals-painted in light color

similar to that produced by the light painted woodwork against the dark brick of so many Queen Anne houses in London. When eclecticism in architecture set in, architects discovered that, with the help of the cheap, precast details, they could imitate any style. Fine textural effects and distinctive forms were no longer appreciated. The architects were quite satisfied if, with the help

of easily recognized details, they could get their buildings to resemble historical prototypes. And then, after a few decades of
employing this borrowed and meaningless ornament, they turned
in protest against all pre-cast banalities and demanded honest
materials and the closest agreement between material and form.

It was, as already indicated, a moral and moralizing tendency.
We find it still being expressed in the advice to architectural students given in 1919 by the Danish architect P. V. Jensen-Klint.

"Cultivate brick, the red or the yellowish-white. Utilize all of
its many possibilities. Use few or no shaped bricks. Do not copy
details, whether Greek or Gothic. Make them yourself from the
material. Do not believe that stucco is a building material, and smile
when your professor says that 'paint is also a material.' If you ever
get a chance to build a house of granite, remember that it is a
precious stone, and if ferro-concrete becomes a building material
do not rest until a new style is found for it."

"For the style is created by the material, the subject, the time,
and the man."

Ferro-concrete did become a building material—first for great
bridges with mighty arched spans. Originally these impressive
structures were seen simply as gray patterns in the midst of Nature's greenery, of the same category as highways and other engi-
neering works. Their textural effect, which is difficult to perceive
from a distance, made no impression. In this way the great grain
elevators rising high above the plains of Nebraska are accepted
almost as part of the landscape. But when cement structures are
placed next to "real" buildings, it becomes immediately apparent
what poor stuff cement is, and many attempts have been made
during the past ten years to produce concrete buildings of a more
attractive textural quality.

Frank Lloyd Wright was one of the early designers of houses
built entirely of reinforced concrete elements. Instead of making
them smooth he gave them deep relief. This may have been due
to his predilection for ornament but nevertheless it helped to
improve the rather amorphous quality of the ferro-concrete.

As a general rule it may be said that materials with poor textural effects are improved by deep relief while materials of high quality can stand a smooth surface and, in fact, appear to best advantage without relief or ornament. Incidentally, it is difficult to differentiate entirely between the impressions of texture and color. White concrete, for example, is not as unattractive as gray but it is best when given structural character, either by using relief moulds or by casting it in formwork made of rough boards. One of the handsomest concrete structures in Denmark is a water tower just outside of Copenhagen, designed in 1928 by Ib Lunding. The walls were cast in formwork made of rough boards one meter long and the imprints they left form a faint relief over the entire structure while horizontal mouldings, a meter apart, hide the joints. From a distance you see only the huge, projecting ribs but as you come closer the gray cement surface comes to life. On the base of the

Close-up view of water tower in Brønshøj showing textural character of concrete which was cast against rough boards

tower the marks of the formwork were smoothed away—probably with the idea of making it finer. But the result is that it seems a dead thing compared to the vital structure above it.

Le Corbusier's early concrete houses were rather poor texturally, particularly those which had to be built cheaply. At that time he painted the concrete surfaces but his later buildings owe their effect less to color than to a robust textural quality. This is particularly true of the huge piers which support the Marseilles block. Their rough concrete surface has a powerful pattern left by the rough boards of the wooden formwork. The ceiling of the church in Ronchamp is also of unpainted concrete of a similar coarse character in striking contrast to the white plastered walls.

Thorvaldsen's dictum that casts are death is, thus, in full accordance with experience gathered in architecture. Castings can be deadly dull when they have not been given an interesting

From Le Corbusier's tall block in Marseille. Note the characteristic surface of the gray concrete pillars which was produced by casting in rough wooden formwork

View of roof terrace atop Le Corbusier's Marseille block

surface pattern or a coat of paint. But what about marble? Is it, as he claimed, resurrection? It is true that a form which is crude and lifeless in cement can be beautiful and vital in a crystalline material. But it depends entirely upon how the stone is treated, what sort of surface it has.

Even a hard, nonporous stone can be employed in such a way as to give no visual idea of form. Marble can be hewn so that its surface becomes sugar-like. The individual crystals sparkle and light penetrates a bit below the surface so that it is impossible to get an exact impression of the form. And in architecture it is distinctly unpleasant when the stone that is supposed to form firm supporting elements seems insecure and almost intangible.

Packed ice in the Sound between Sweden and Denmark. Under the ice is shingle, stones which have been smoothed and rounded by the action of the water

This is not meant as a general condemnation of what I have called a sugar-like surface. We all enjoy a landscape of ice-blocks gleaming white with deep blue shadows, composed entirely of sparkling crystals so loosely combined that the rays of the sun penetrate and create strange, green reflections behind screens of crystal-clear icicles. Fairy tale palaces may be built of ice, but for buildings in our more prosaic world firm textural effects are necessary—the kind that are found *under* the ice in cobblestones, which are just as everlasting as the ice landscape's fata morgana is transitory.

Cobblestones, which for aeons have rubbed against each other, are ideally smooth. They are firm and pleasant to the touch, smooth and definitive in form, absolutely precise in textural effect. Granite flagstones which have been worn smooth by the feet of generations of walkers have the same character. By being polished, stone can be made to shine even more, but the only result is that the surface becomes less precise. The Danish architect, Carl Petersen, has explained why this is so. An outer, glass-like layer is formed which most of the light penetrates until it is stopped a little below the surface by stone particles that form a more uneven layer. In other words, two surfaces are seen at the same time: an outer reflecting one and a rough inner one. This produces the same flickering double effect that we find in a snapshot taken as the camera moved. The same effect is found in polished wood. We have all seen highly polished table tops which look as though they were wet or covered with glass. It is not the fact that the surface is mirror-like that is unpleasant—metal does not give a double effect no matter how highly polished it is.

At various times and in the most diverse civilizations efforts have been made to create perfectly smooth, firm surfaces. In ancient times the Egyptians and Greeks produced smoothly polished sculpture of unsurpassed beauty. And in distant countries where fine old traditions are kept up you can find even the most utilitarian articles of porcelain, stoneware, wood, or lacquer, as smooth and precise in textural character as the pebbles of the sea. This was my own experience in a little Chinese town several decades ago. But when modern civilization comes to these countries gimcrack, trashy things often follow in its wake. You see them in cheap shops under glaring electric lights: gaudy mirrors, vulgar radio cabinets of glossy veneer, fantastic bric-a-brac and all the rest. How bogus and ugly they are compared to the simple, genuine articles in the shop next door!

This is by no means the fault of the machine, as is so often claimed. On the contrary, machines have helped man to produce forms and surfaces nearer perfection than anything found in Nature or produced by hand. Such, for example, are the steel balls in ball-bearings. Le Corbusier has sung the praise of such mathematically perfect products though he does not employ them himself. His forte is more the inspired and inspiring sketch than the precisely worked out definitive thing.

But other modernists work with cool, smooth forms—Mies van der Rohe, for instance, and Marcel Breuer—in interiors which are sometimes as sterile as operating rooms. In Berlin, between the two wars, the architects Luckhardt and Anker built houses with façades entirely of glass and chromium-plated steel.

A building of elegant and interesting textural qualities was designed in 1937 by the Danish architect Arne Jacobsen for a paint firm in Copenhagen. It is a ferro-concrete building with faced walls. The outer walls of the two lower floors are covered with sand-blasted iron-plating painted a lusterless color so that it looks as though it were made all of one piece. The walls of the upper floors are faced with handsomely glazed gray tiles. Thus, the same façade has four surface elements: painted iron, glazed tile, chromium-plated metal and glass. Though dissimilar, they go very well together. All four are cool and precise. Jacobsen's building shows the same conception of urban architecture as that demonstrated in the Regent Street houses in London with their smoothly painted façades.

After the second world war American architects began to employ the same textural effects that their European colleagues had worked with between the wars. Building after building appeared in American cities made of glass and steel. And from America these textural effects have returned to Europe as the very latest style in American architecture.

The experimental architects who cultivated smooth materials also worked with rough ones, such as wood in its natural state, coarsely hewn stone and undisguised structures. They were eager to try every possibility of striking textural effects from the smooth and elegant to the coarse and rustic.

In *Staatliches Bauhaus*, 1919 (later continued in *Bauhaus Dessau*), Walter Gropius developed a school of modern architecture and design. Here, new methods were introduced to train the senses to a higher degree of awareness than in ordinary schools. The Bauhaus wished to avoid conventional architectural thinking and to liberate the creative capacity of its students. Instead of

Walter Gropius: Buildings for Bauhaus, Dessau. Planned 1925. The textural effects produced by the light smooth walls and great areas of glass were new at that time

listening to lectures on traditional methods of employing materials they were to learn for themselves through their own experiments. By recording their impressions of the various materials they worked with, the students gathered a compendium of valuable information for future use. Emphasis was laid not simply on the appearance of surfaces but particularly on the feel of them. The tactile sense was trained in experiments with textures systematically arranged according to degree of coarseness. By running their fingers over the materials again and again, the students were finally able to sense a sort of musical scale of textural values. Materials used were wood treated in various ways, a variety of textiles, and paper with different reliefs.

The school claimed—undoubtedly with justice—that the civilized European had lost something of primitive man's sensitive awareness of textural surfaces and believed that by training this sense a foundation could be laid for the production of things of high textural quality.

The Bauhaus people were inspired by the experiments of contemporary painters with compositions of bits of wood, paper and cloth. But they could have found the same inspiration in their own art. Before Bauhaus, architecture had often sought renewal through interesting combinations of materials, both natural and artificial. For thousands of years man has worked with wood in all its guises, from logs in their natural state to smoothly planed and polished timber, and has taken advantage of its many varieties of color and organic structure in combination with many forms of technique.

In the old English walnut chair, opposite, from about 1700, the organic structure of the wood has in some strange way become one with the chair. The chair-maker so skillfully utilized the grain pattern in his design that it forms a symmetrical ornament in the saddle-like seat and makes the beautifully shaped arm even more vital and natural. The same masterly employment of wood is sometimes found in architecture. There are old half-timber houses in which every piece of wood seems to have been carefully chosen for the particular spot where it is used; straight pieces are all uprights, crooked ones brackets and curved struts. But such buildings are exceptions. Usually there is a certain contrast between the organic grain pattern and the geometry of carpentry.

When wood is exposed to wind and weather its grain pattern stands out more clearly. The pith in the wood is worn off and washed away so that the pattern stands in relief. At the same time the wood changes color. Yellow, resinous sorts become silvery gray. They are like old people whose wrinkled and weather-beaten faces have more character than young faces. In countries where there are many old wooden houses the special beauty of weathered wood becomes very apparent. In English country houses built

Detail of English walnut chair from about 1700

A.C.Schweinfurth: Unitarian
Church, Berkeley, California.
Details which show the textural effects. Above, wall
shingles seen behind the boughs
of a vistaria. Below, corner
post consisting of the trunk of
a redwood still covered with
its loose, soft bark

during the last century weathered oak was combined very effectively with stone or red brick. And in the same century, in America, H. H. Richardson, in his search for interesting materials,
used wooden shingles as a wall facing as did also McKim, Meade
and White on the walls of large, romantic country houses. A generation later these textural effects were again the fashion. B. R. Maybeck built wooden houses for the University of California and
its neighborhood which fit in naturally with the luxuriant vegeta-
tion of the surrounding slopes. Not far from Maybeck's houses
another American—A. C. Schweinfurth—erected a Unitarian
church for which he used the rough trunks of redwood trees as
corner posts and coarse shingling for the walls. The thick, loose

bark forms a vivid contrast to the smoother surface of the shingles.
The architectural firm of Greene and Greene also worked with
robust materials. They built country houses with outer walls of
vitrified, twisted bricks and with brackets and corbels of massive
woodwork that is faintly reminiscent of Japanese architecture.
The interiors were as elegant as the exteriors were rustic. In one
of them the architects employed golden mahogany—not a veneer
but the massive wood—whole blocks and beams of it, rounded
and polished but not profiled. The woodwork is joined by visible
pegs and dowels so that the timber construction is exposed and
the organic structure of every piece of wood is clearly seen. The
woodwork in this house is like fine furniture, beautiful to look at
and pleasant to touch.

*Detail of
staircase in
private house,
built by Greene
& Greene on
Piedmont
Avenue in
Berkeley,
California. All
woodwork is
of massive
mahogany in
a lovely
golden hue*

Medieval masonry of large bricks

Modern masonry of yellow brick
Knud Hansen, Architect

Materials are judged not only by their surface appearance but also according to their hardness and their heat-conducting ability. Those which may become very cold or very hot are equally unpleasant. Wood is a sympathetic material because it never has a temperature shock in store for us.

In Japanese gardens there are tiles and stepping stones designed to be walked on with wooden clogs. These the Japanese takes off when he enters his house where the floors are covered with matting and everything made of wood and paper and other friendly materials that are sympathetic to the touch. Posts are likely to have the natural form of tree trunks or branches that have been barked and smoothly turned, and the wall covering adapts itself to their every contour. There are all kinds of plaited materials from the finest basket weave to plaited shavings as broad as webbing. Compared to the sensitively designed Japanese house many of our modern buildings are amazingly crude. They may have certain Japanese reminiscences and be built of the same materials, but not only do outdoor materials creep in over the floor in the shape of rough-hewn stone, but indoor walls, too, are often of the most rustic character, such as cyclopean walls of undressed granite

Medieval masonry,
Roskilde Cathedral, Denmark

18th century masonry, Frederik V's chapel,
Roskilde Cathedral

or clinker walls with scraped joints. Where the Japanese seek to unite the various organic materials, the western architect often seems to shatter unity and create crass contrasting effects.

Turning now to masonry, we find that it too has its problems. It is possible to build a house of stones that have been so accurately cut to fit together that they do not require filling material between them but simply rest on each other, held together by their own weight. Thus, the columns of Greek temples were constructed of stone or marble blocks placed one on top of the other with no filling between. And this is still done today when a perfectly homogeneous textural effect is desired, as in the case of the columns on the façade of the Faaborg art museum in Denmark. But most masonry is a combination of two materials—two very dissimilar materials at that—such as fired brick and mortar made of lime mixed with sand and water. As there are many kinds of brick and many kinds of mortar that can be combined, and as the final result also depends on the jointing and the pattern of the bond, it will be understood that there are an infinite number of possibilities. Different civilizations and different periods are characterized by particular types of brickwork but all of them

Alvar Aalto: Baker House at M.I.T. Note the characteristic brickwork

are composed of the same simple elements: brick and mortar. The brick is always regarded as the actual building material, the mortar simply as filling. Brick, therefore, should not only form the larger percentage of the wall surface but its material and color should dominate; it should appear coarser and stronger than the filling. If a fine, smooth brick is used the mortar must be equally fine. The architects of the Greek Revival were aware of this. Though they preferred stone walls, when they did use bricks they were small and well formed, smooth but not too hard, and walled up with very thin joints of fine mortar. This is clearly seen when we compare the two illustrations from Roskilde Cathedral where the Danish kings are buried, one showing part of the wall of the medieval nave, the other the brickwork of Frederik V's chapel from the end of the eighteenth century. Very similar brickwork is found in eighteenth century buildings in other countries. The façade walls in Louisburg Square, in Boston, for instance, are almost the same as the walls of Frederik V's chapel.

When building costs permit, architects usually prefer handmade brick which, within the limits of the rigid technique, give life and character to walls. It is obtainable in many varieties, from the very coarse clinker brick used by Aalto with deeply recessed joints for the walls of Baker House at M.I.T., to the soft, light-colored brick which has been used by the Danish architect Arne Jacobsen for most of his newer buildings.

CHAPTER VIII

Daylight in Architecture

Daylight is constantly changing. The other elements of architecture we have considered can be exactly determined. The architect can fix the dimensions of solids and cavities, he can designate the orientation of his building, he can specify the materials and the way they are to be treated; he can describe precisely the quantities and qualities he desires in his building before a stone has been laid. Daylight alone he cannot control. It changes from morning to evening, from day to day, both in intensity and color. How is it possible to work with such a capricious factor? How can it be utilized artistically?

Illustration above shows market hall in Cadillac

First of all, variations in the quantity of light can be ignored, for though they can be measured with the help of instruments, we ourselves are hardly aware of them. The adaptability of the human eye is surprisingly great. Bright sunlight may be 250,000 times more intense than moonlight and yet we can see the same forms in the light of the moon as we can in broad daylight. The amount of light reflected from a white surface in winter is less than that reflected from a black surface of the same size in summer but still we see the white as white and the black as black. And we can clearly distinguish a black letter on a white ground.

Light is of decisive importance in experiencing architecture. The same room can be made to give very different spatial impressions by the simple expedient of changing the size and location of its openings. Moving a window from the middle of a wall to a corner will utterly transform the entire character of the room.

To avoid becoming lost in the multitude of possibilities, we will here confine ourselves to three types: the bright open hall, the room with a skylight and, most typical of all, the room with light entering from the side.

We can find examples from many periods of the open hall with light coming in on all sides, particularly in countries with warm climates. It consists simply of a roof supported on columns for protection from the burning sun. For our example I have chosen a covered market in the town of Cadillac, near Bordeaux, in southern France. It has a very high ceiling, much higher than in the houses surrounding the market-place. The hall is accessible from all four sides and is very light, full of reflections from the yellow pavement outside. But nevertheless the light inside the hall is different from that outdoors. When wares are on display near the arched openings, they receive a great deal of direct light on one side while the other lies in shadow. But the shady side is never really dark, the entire hall is too light for that. All in all, the light on a cloudy day is more concentrated inside the hall than in the open, and much brighter than in most enclosed rooms. At various times architects have tried to create enclosed rooms with this kind of lighting. There are medieval castles with large windows in both side walls and in innumerable manor houses there is one large room running through the house from one outer wall to the other with windows on either side. Coming from one of the smaller rooms, with windows in one wall only, into this huge room flooded with light gives a feeling of relief for it is so bright and airy.

Today, when we have better means than ever before of creating this type of room, it is seldom seen. There is, however, an excellent example of it in the house which Philip C. Johnson built for himself in New Canaan, Connecticut. It consists of one large cell, a rectangular room about twice as long as it is broad, with glass walls on all four sides and a solid roof. The bathroom is in a brick cylinder reaching from floor to ceiling which stands in the middle of the room, and the kitchen consists simply of several low wooden cabinets fixed to the brick floor. From a picture of the house it is hard to imagine that an indoor feeling can be created in such a transparent glass box. But experienced from inside the effect is quite different. It is definitely an indoor room. The floor and ceiling help to give a feeling of an interior and the textiles and the grouping of the furniture add to the indoor atmosphere. From ceiling to floor the glass walls are provided with curtains or white screens which can be moved back and forth to control the light and keep out inquisitive glances. These also help to strengthen the indoor feeling. The Japanese system of sliding walls has here been transferred from a house of wood and paper to one of steel and glass.

Outdoors the light sifts through the foliage of trees scattered about the grounds. You gaze out *under* their branches at the view and you feel—just as in one of Palladio's villas—that here you have a firm base, a carefully conceived plan, from which to observe the surrounding countryside seen through the rectangles of the steel framework. The main group of furniture, standing on a large rug, is well placed in a zone between the center of the room and the south wall. Here, too, in an excellent light, are a large piece of sculpture and an easel holding a modern painting.

Living room in house built for himself by Philip C. Johnson. New Canaan, Connecticut

Before going further, it would be well to explain what I mean by "an excellent light." It is necessary because to most people a good light means only much light. If we do not see a thing well enough we simply demand *more* light. And very often we find that it does not help because the *quantity* of light is not nearly as important as its *quality*.

Let us imagine that we are looking at a projecting corner formed by the meeting of two white planes. If the two planes are evenly illuminated from sources that can be controlled, the light can be so regulated that the two sides will look equally light. When this happens the edge of the corner can no longer be observed by the eye. You may still recognize it because of the stereoscopic character of your eyes or because you can see where the two planes intersect other planes. But you will have lost an essential means of seeing that there *is* a corner. It will not help to increase the light if it is increased equally on both sides. But if the light on one of the sides is reduced so that there will be a decided difference in the lighting of the two planes, the corner will clearly emerge even if the total intensity of light has now become lower.

From this it should be clear why a "front light" is generally a poor light. When light falls on a relief at almost a right angle, there will be a minimum of shadow and therefore of plastic effect. The textural effect will also be poor, simply because perception of texture depends on minute differences in relief. If the object is moved from front light to a place where light falls on it from the side, it will be possible to find a spot which gives a particularly good impression both of relief and of texture. A good photographer will continue to experiment until he finds exactly the right light for his subject. If the lighted parts are too light the form on that side is killed, and if the parts in shadow are too dark no form will be seen there. Therefore he chooses a light which gives many variations, from the brightest high light to the deepest shadow, variations which bring out the true plasticity of every rounded part. He arranges for a suitable amount of reflected light among the shadows to obtain relief there also. When he finally has adjusted the light so that it gives a completely plastic picture of his subject and an accurate account of its texture, with no vague spots, he says that his picture is well lighted.

The quality of light is much more important than is generally recognized. Those who do fine work, such as needlework, soon become tired if the light is poor, and too often they try—in vain—to remedy it by increasing the intensity of the light instead of the quality.

The concert hall in Gothenburg, Sweden, has a long public foyer on the second floor with a window extending almost the entire length of the side wall. The hall is painted in light colors and there is plenty of reflected light from walls and ceiling. At one end the wall is entirely covered by a colorful woven tapestry which receives side light coming from the window at the left. This location does full justice to the design, texture and colors of the handsome tapestry. The fact that it is not evenly lighted over the entire surface is irrelevant inasmuch as the tapestry is meant to be seen not as an isolated work of art but as an integral part of the room. If it were hung on a wall with front light it would in fact be impossible to see that the picture is woven.

Ed. Degas: Dancers. Showing the special magic of footlights

The old-fashioned stage footlights were flattering to costumes and scenery while the richer lighting effects of the modern stage often kill all beauty. In the old days the light on the actors came from below, which, as a matter of fact, is not good because we are used to light coming from above. It was a topsy-turvy world with the parts that usually lie in shadow bathed in light and those that are usually lit up, lying in shadow. We have all seen these lighting effects in paintings by Degas and Toulouse-Lautrec where light falls on the under side of noses and chins. This sort of illumination became a convention of the theater, and when the footlights went on they immediately created that atmosphere of enchantment and unreality which is the world of the stage. The essential thing about them is that they actually did produce shadows so that the audience was not cheated of textural effects. In the modern theater, on the other hand, the principal actors are often so lavishly bathed in

spotlights that you might well think that the experiment, mentioned above, with equally lighted sides of a projecting corner was
being made. The faces of the actors appear as blobs of light with
all features blotted out. In such illumination even the richest
materials appear flat and shoddy. The lighting of the modern
stage proves conclusively that it is not the amount of light which
matters. The important thing is the way the light falls.

After this long digression it should be clear that there are places
in Philip Johnson's house admirably suited for the display of art,
and others—with an equal amount of light entering from two
sides—that are much less suitable. In the furnishing of the room
this has been taken into account and as a result you sit in good
light and see the works of art under the most favorable conditions.
And at the same time you can enjoy the view on all sides.

The antithesis of such a room, which is closed at the top and
open on the sides, is the room which is closed on all sides and
open at the top. The former offers a variety of lighting effects in
different parts of the room while the latter can be planned so that
the light is equally good in all parts of the room.

The most beautiful example of an entirely enclosed interior
lighted from above is the Pantheon in Rome. No picture can do it
justice because it is the great architecturally enclosed space round
us which makes the deepest impression, not any sectional view.
Coming into the Pantheon from the tangled network of streets
outside, we experience it as the perfect expression of peace and
harmony. The ordinary scale of the houses just passed makes
the peristyle, in comparison, seem overwhelmingly high with
its gigantic columns disappearing into the twilight under the
roof. As you enter the rotunda you are immediately aware of a
mild light coming from a source high above you, three times as
high as the ceiling of the peristyle. The dome does not seem to
limit the space but rather to expand and raise it.

The rotunda is as large and spacious as a Roman piazza. At no
point do the walls thrust forward; the great mass of masonry
forms a perfect circle around the enormous room. The dome is a

Sectional drawing of the Pantheon, Rome. From Desgodetz

hemisphere which is so high up that if it were to continue down to a whole sphere it would just touch the floor. In other words, the height of the wall cylinder is equal to the radius of the dome, the height of the room equal to its width and breadth. This harmony of form corresponds to something great and ideal in the execution of the edifice, and especially in its lighting. The circular opening at the summit of the dome forms the only connection with the outside world—not with the noisy, casual world of the streets but with a still greater hemisphere, the celestial sky above it. When the sun does not enter in a slanting cylinder of rays, the light is finely diffused because it comes from such a great height. But it all falls in the same direction, coming from a single source and producing real shadows. The floor, beautifully paved in a pattern of squares and circles of marble, receives most of the light and enough is reflected to brighten even the darkest spots so that there are no really black shadows anywhere. The wall recesses and tabernacles, with their Corinthian columns and cornices, receive enough light to bring out the architectonic forms in full plasticity. The Pantheon's magnificent rotunda has often been copied in other dimensions. But this disturbs the entire balance and harmony of the room, especially if the size of the light opening is also changed or if extra openings are added in the walls.

It is also remarkable to see how different the lighting effect becomes when the same section is employed on a rectangular ground plan so that the dome becomes a barrel vault with an oblong instead of a round opening. This can be seen in Copenhagen's cathedral built in Greek Revival. It has a long, barrel-vaulted nave with three light openings in the vaulting. The proportion between the dimensions of the light openings and the floor is about the same as in the Pantheon and therefore the light is not any stronger. But for some reason or other, the effect produced by the three openings is of one long groove of light running through the nave rather than of three pools of concentrated light. Thorvaldsen's statues of the disciples, which line the walls, receive not only direct light but also light from both sides and the result is that the entire interior seems excessively light and lacking in character.

The chancel is lighted by a fourth opening in the roof which is hidden from the eye of the congregation and therefore has a rather theatrical effect. In many churches, particularly modern ones, the architect has sought to create a gradual increase in light towards the altar. In the Faaborg Art Museum in Denmark a very rich effect has been produced by doing just the opposite. A climax is created by letting a small dimly lighted room follow a brilliantly lighted one. In the museum the first room, with its large skylight, is as bright as day. Seen from it the octagonal domed hall is like a mystic sanctuary. A dim light sifts down from the small opening in the dome over the black stone statue of the founder, Mads Rasmussen. The impressive figure turns towards the observer and the light is just enough to reveal the great form from which the sculptor, Kai Nielsen, has smoothed away all but the essential. The statue is seen against a cobalt blue wall, the color of which is strangely intensified in the half-light of the hall. (See

Ragnar Östberg: The Blue Hall, Stockholm's city hall
The picture shows that high side-light gives a relatively dim but interesting light

illustration p. 223 showing the opposite view, from the twilit blue hall towards the bright red picture gallery.) If the hall were lighter the effect would be much less dramatic.

There are many examples of rooms in which the entire ceiling is one large skylight. This free influx of natural light gives a shadowless interior; forms are not quite plastic and textural effects are generally poor. This can be seen in Copenhagen's city hall which has two courts—an open one and a glass-roofed one, the main hall of the building. Though you would expect the light in

E. G. Asplund: City hall in Gothenburg, Sweden. The large window facing outer court.
To avoid harsh shadows the steel shafts were covered and given soft contours

both places to be much the same, there is actually an amazing difference. The hall is dull and lifeless. When Ragnar Östberg was
planning Stockholm's city hall he visited Nyrop's in Copenhagen
and learned something from both its good and bad qualities. His
building also has an open and a covered court but, instead of
giving the latter a glass roof, Östberg built a solid ceiling over it
which, on three sides, rests on bands of windows. In this way he
obtained high side lighting immediately under the ceiling and
though the entire hall is darker than Nyrop's, the lighting is
more interesting, not so shadowless and dead. When we turn
from Stockholm to Gothenburg, we again find a city hall with a

E. G. Asplund: City hall in Gothenburg. All daylight comes from the same direction, partly from the left through the large window shown on the opposite page, partly from windows in the ceiling

covered and an open court. But here the architect, Asplund, chose to connect the two by giving the hall a glass wall out towards the open court. Thus, daylight enters this hall from the side. But as the glass wall could be only two stories high and the hall itself is three stories high and quite deep, Asplund found it necessary to supplement the glass wall with an opening in the roof. It is not an ordinary skylight but more like a single section of a saw-tooth roof so that the light here also comes from the side, and, of course, the same side as the light entering through the glass wall. This arrangement gives a very satisfactory light which does full justice to the fine materials in the building.

From the lighting method employed in the Gothenburg city hall it is only a short step to the room lighted by side light alone. Probably the most instructive examples of this are to be found in old Dutch houses, which are unique of their kind. The purely physical conditions of the land in Holland were so special that they led to a novel building method. In many towns the houses were built on reclamed land. While in other countries land was simply something that was there, in Holland the people often had to create it themselves. Every square foot was the result of hard and costly labor and therefore it was necessary to use it with the strictest economy. Before building could begin many piles had to be driven into the ground for each wall. The result of all this was limited land and densely built houses rising high into the air rather than spreading out on the ground. In some towns the costliness of the land is literally illustrated by the fact that the tall houses expand towards the top so that the upper stories project far out over the streets. Thus the typical old Dutch house was a deep, tall, narrow gabled building. The lower floors were used for dwelling purposes, the upper for storage of goods, thus making it possible to concentrate a great deal within a small area. To procure enough light for the dwelling the lower part of the gabled front was pierced by many large window openings. The deep side walls were often shared with the neighboring houses so that there could be no openings in them. All light had to come from the windows in front and rear. Structurally this was ideal because the side walls supported the floor beams and roof while the gable ends had nothing to support but themselves. The front consisted of a rather thin brick wall above and of wood and glass below. Earlier, glass had been so expensive and difficult to procure that the lower —and larger—part of the windows was equipped with shutters only, while the upper part had fixed leaded panes. In good weather the shutters could be kept open so that the inhabitants could look out and the light flood in. But in bad weather the light which came through the small panes above had to suffice. Later, the lower half of the windows was also glazed but the shutters were retained

16th century houses in Vere, Holland, showing the large window space; fixed panes above, wooden shutters below

and the new panes fitted into casement frames which opened inward. Sometimes the upper part was also equipped with shutters, in which case they opened into the room. This produced a four-framed window with a shutter to each frame that could be opened or closed independently so that the light could be regulated at will.

It is easy to see the relation between the difficult land problem, the narrow houses, and the location of the windows in the end walls. It is also understandable that there had to be a great deal of window space to procure enough light for the deep interiors. But none of this explains why the Dutch took a much greater interest in the windows of their houses and the regulation of daylight than did the people of any other country. After they had perfected their four-shutter system they even went further, adding curtains and hangings. Old paintings of Dutch interiors show that heavy draperies were used as well as thin glass curtains, which softened the transition from the dark window pier to the light opening.

Dutch interiors of the period must have been very different
from Italian or French interiors. The probable explanation is
that the rich Dutch merchants, who lived in a harsher climate,
stayed indoors more than the Southerners and therefore were
more interested in the furnishing of their homes than in the form
of the rooms themselves, which were so important especially to
Italians. At any rate, the Dutch merchants were good judges of
merchandise and materials and filled their houses with costly
rugs and porcelain from the Orient, bought heavy, handsome
furniture and had their clothes made of the best materials. And,
as we have already seen, it is necessary to have good lighting to
enjoy textural effects.

How much the ordinary burgher used the shutters it is difficult
to say. But we have abundant evidence that the Dutch painters of
the seventeenth century took full advantage of the many lighting
possibilities the special Dutch building method offered. The
lower floors in most houses had very high ceilings. On the ground

Restored house in Delft with original windows; fixed panes above and shutters and inward-opening casement windows below

Room in the house in Delft shown above. The window is right up against the side wall giving bright and high side-light. Shutters are closed

floor in Rembrandt's house the height from floor to ceiling beam was 14 feet. The rooms with their white plastered walls and large windows could be as drenched with light as the rooms in the most modern house today. But the light could also be dimmed down

Jan Vermeer van Delft:
Interior showing man
and woman standing
next to a clavichord.
Buckingham Palace

to a most mysterious gloom. Or all of it could be concentrated on one spot, leaving the rest of the room in semi-darkness. No one has employed these effects with greater skill than Rembrandt, as his paintings show. They also show the wealth of textural effects that could be produced by this special lighting method.

But it is in Jan Vermeer's paintings that the lighting of Dutch interiors is best documented. Many of his pictures were painted in a room with windows stretching from one side wall to the other. Vermeer worked experimentally with the problems of natural light. His easel almost always stood in the same spot, with light coming from the left, and his usual background was a white-washed wall parallel with the picture surface. In some of his paint-ings you see no more of the room than that one wall but never-theless you are conscious of the entire room because it is reflected in the objects depicted. You are aware of the strong light coming from the left and reflections from the other walls give light and

Jan Vermeer:
The Pearl Weigher.
Philadelphia

color to the shadows, which are never colorless. Even when the painting shows only one figure against a light rear wall you experience an entire room. In a famous Vermeer at Buckingham Palace, depicting two persons standing by a musical instrument, you see his studio as it appeared when all of the shutters were open. The windows are typically Dutch with fixed panes above and casement frames below fitted with colored glass. The rearmost window is right up against the wall and the light coming through it produces marked shadows of furniture and pictures on that wall. They are softened by reflected light and especially by light coming from the other windows. The picture shows exactly how the shadows recede, not gradually but in stages, in as much as each window casts its own distinctly outlined shadow. If we take this as the basic picture and compare other Vermeers with it, we can see exactly what happened when all or part of one or more of the windows was darkened. The paintings are such accurate studies

that it is possible to determine exactly how the shutters were arranged for each picture. For example, in the Philadelphia Vermeer of the girl weighing pearls, the light comes from the upper half of the rearmost window alone and it is further dimmed by curtains. The frame on the wall casts a deep shadow—and only one shadow. In other Vermeer pictures it is the rearmost window which is darkened. In this way you can go through all of his paintings and determine just how he obtained the right light for each picture.

Vermeer's contemporary Pieter de Hooch also worked with natural light but in more complicated motives. In his paintings you very often look from one room into another and from one light to another. But the form of each room is clear and simple and the light in each is very distinct so that there are no ambiguous zones in his pictures.

In present-day Holland windows with this unique shutter system can be seen only in old houses that have been restored to their original form. But such houses do exist (see illustrations pages 199—201) and in them you can observe the innumerable possibilities the system offered for the regulation of light.

A few years ago, at the School of Architecture in Copenhagen, we reconstructed the old Dutch illumination control and studied the various effects it allowed. Charlottenborg, in which the school is housed, is a typical large Dutch mansion of the seventeenth century. The second floor windows are twice as high as they are broad and are divided in four lights of equal size. By equipping each pane with solid shutters we were able to regulate daylight as they did in the old Dutch houses. We used the windows in one of the large square rooms for our experiment and learned a great deal from it. Shutting the lower halves only, we produced a more even light over the entire room; by darkening the upper halves and leaving the lower unshuttered, the light was concentrated near the windows. We were able to create the most dramatic Rembrandt chiaroscuro and to reproduce Vermeer's lighting arrangements. When the free-hand drawing class worked in this room we experimented with the shutters until we found the

Interior from Goldoni's house in Venice with window placed in typical Venetian fashion up against side wall

*Interior from
Kronborg
Castle,
Denmark.
Example of
the lighting
effects in old
buildings with
thick walls
which Elis
Benckert was
interested in*

light which would best bring out the plastic qualities and textural characteristics of the model that was being copied. All in all,
the old Dutch shutter system taught us something about the
effects the architect can produce by the skillful utilization of
daylight. In Venetian houses, as already mentioned, it is not unusual
to have rooms containing two windows separated as far as possible
by a solid stretch of wall. In the old palaces there was often a deep
central room behind an open loggia, and on either side of this
summer room were the winter rooms with the far-separated windows. In this way each room had a characteristic light that was
flattering to paintings and sculpture. Outside of Venice and the
Dutch towns architects have seldom worked with lighting effects
of this kind. A few examples, however, can be found.

In 1910 the Swedish architect, Elis Benckert (1881–1913) built
a villa in a suburb of Stockholm in which there were several very
unusually placed windows. Today, unfortunately, most of the

Elis Benckert:
Interior from
Villa
Lagerkrantz
in Djursholm
near
Stockholm.
Note how
window splay
is carried into
the room as a
light reflector

original ideas in the design have been destroyed by rebuilding. Benckert had studied the lighting in old Swedish buildings with thick walls, windows against side walls and deep reveals. He utilized the experience thus gathered in his design of the dining room where the reveal was continued in the side wall. This threw a fine light on the large tapestry which hung on that wall.

In the beginning, Functionalism was more a matter of slogans than of definite solutions to problems of design and structure. Such words as *free*, *open* and *light* were the keynotes of the new style. Too often, however, it was quantity of light rather than quality which was sought. But Le Corbusier, who is a painter and sculptor as well as an architect, has from the very beginning designed rooms in which the light comes from one side through windows covering an entire wall. This could give as fine light to the room as in an old Dutch house but Le Corbusier's windows often lack means of regulating the light. The light in the large room of the apartments in his Marseilles block recalls the loggia rooms in a Venetian palace. The ceiling is very high and the window opening takes up an entire wall. Where the old houses had a mass of fine stone detail, such as columns, arches and lace-like tracery, Le Corbusier's has concrete grillwork. And he has sought to regulate the light so that comparatively much penetrates deep into the room. The side walls are well lighted and everything in the room has the crystal clarity he so admires.

One of the problems with which modern architects are often faced is to obtain good, even lighting for many different parts of a large room. Skylighting is not so good because the light from it is much too diffused to produce the shadows necessary to see form and texture clearly and easily. Neither is side light alone satisfactory for, though much better, it does not penetrate deeply enough. The answer has been found in the saw-tooth roof, i. e. a series of high side lights which produce an excellent light in all parts of the room. The same problem arises in schoolroom design: how to provide even lighting for all of the desks in the room. Here, a wrong solution is often employed by supplementing a primary row of windows in one wall with a secondary one high up in the opposite wall. This is used especially in England where so much emphasis is placed on cross-ventilation. From a lighting standpoint it is not good. Windows high up in a rear wall give no direct light to that wall or to the part of the room nearest to it, which is the darkest part. On the other hand, they create a middle zone further ahead which receives an almost equal amount of light from both sides, which is, of course, undesirable. Inquiries that have been made among the pupils in such classrooms show that there are certain desks which the children—without being able to say why—do not like to work at.

A more or less concentrated light—that is, light from one or more sources falling in the same direction—is the best in which to see form and texture. At the same time it emphasizes the closed character of a room. Light alone can create the effect of enclosed space. A campfire on a dark night forms a cave of light circum-

Le Corbusier: Church in Ronchamps, Haute Saone, France

scribed by a wall of darkness. Those who are within the circle of light have the secure feeling of being together in the same room. It follows, therefore, that if you wish to create an effect of openness you cannot employ concentrated light. Early in his career Frank Lloyd Wright recognized this. In his houses built on the so-called open plan you find walls and partitions which do not go all the way to the ceiling but leave space for openings at the top. This not only gives an open feeling to the room but it admits extra light. On the whole, however, Wright's interiors are often rather dark, for despite large windows, overhanging eaves and surrounding trees take much of the direct light. And especially the materials he uses

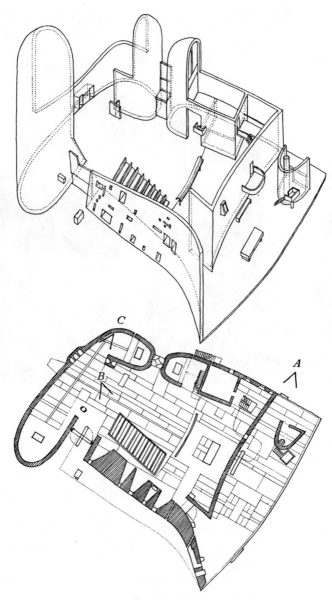

Le Corbusier: Church in Ronchamps
Below, plan. Above, spatial drawing

Le Corbusier: Church in Ronchamps. East side seen from Point A on plan p. 210

*Le Corbusier:
Church in
Ronchamps.
Window wall
seen from
Point B on
plan p. 210*

add to the darkness. He is fond of employing rough and robust effects, rusticated stone and undressed wood, as well as naked walls and thick carpets. With the passing of time they all become dark. For corners which would otherwise lie completely in shadow, hiding interesting textural effects, he procures extra light through a long, low window, a triangular pane of glass, or some other novelty, which brightens up the shadows just as the extra lamps used by professional photographers do. And in this side light the grain pattern of the wood and the geometric carvings can be clearly seen. It is an exceedingly refined art, very deliberately and skilfully employed; but it is dangerous to imitate. Too many houses nowadays are filled with light coming from all directions, without any artistic purpose and creating only a confused glare.

Le Corbusier, who hitherto has worked with daylight-flooded rooms, so well suited to precise forms and pure colors, has created a church interior in Ronchamps which has the emotional appeal

*Le Corbusier:
Church in
Ronchamps.
Interior with
niche seen from
Point C on
plan p. 210*

that is based on the shadowed dimness of indirect lighting, in which form is only vaguely revealed. It is a Catholic shrine dedicated to a miraculous image of the Virgin Mary, and the design of the entire building is based on ideas and emotions entirely different from those which have determined his work hitherto. From a distance, the white walls and tower of the church can be seen dominating the highest summit of a mountain landscape in Haute Saone, where one crest of mountains surges behind another. The undulating rhythm of the landscape seems to continue in the design of the church. As you come nearer you discover that there is not one plane surface; the entire building curves and swells into an extraordinarily well-integrated composition.

On entering the church the first thing that strikes you is that it is very dark. Gradually you become aware of the walls and you begin to realize that plane surfaces and regularity are no more to be found inside the building than on the exterior. The very floor is like an undulating landscape of stone slabs in an irregular pattern. A small group of sturdy pews for the worshippers forms a parallelogram at one side of the room, facing the altar and the Madonna image high above it. This holy relic stands in a glass case let into the thick wall so that it can be seen both from inside the church and from outside where outdoor mass is sometimes held. To the right is a fathom-thick wall pierced by many openings of unequal sizes. From the outside they resemble tiny peepholes but inside they open up into large, white embrasures which cast a great deal of reflected light into the dim-lit room. Some of these openings have been filled with glass on which ornaments or inscriptions are painted. In the angle formed by the south side wall and the end wall containing the Madonna there is a narrow fissure from floor to ceiling with a huge, screen-like arrangement of concrete which apparently is meant to keep out direct light. But, unfortunately, so much light penetrates that it completely dazzles the worshipper who is trying to concentrate on his devotions. The penumbra of the church is cleaved by streaks of radiant light from the narrow fissure. Otherwise only little light enters. Between walls and ceiling there is a very narrow opening which admits just enough light for one to see the rough concrete ceiling against the white plastered walls. What appear on the outside as towers—two towards the east and one towards the west—are seen in the interior as apses, recessed enlargements of the room. And what appear to be belfry lights are actually windows which cannot be seen from the interior but which, from high up above the roof, shed a magic light over the curved walls of the apse so that the worshipper's attention is drawn towards it, towards its altar and up above where the light is brightest.

In this remarkable cult-building Le Corbusier has made a new contribution to architecture and has shown in a striking way what a wonderful means of expression the artist possesses in daylight and its distribution.

CHAPTER IX

Color in Architecture

It is well known that ancient Greek temples were originally poly-chrome but time has robbed them of every trace of color so that today they stand in naked stone. But even though this process must have changed them greatly, we still experience them as noble architecture. When a painting loses its color it no longer exists as a work of art but this is not true of architecture, for the art of building is first and foremost concerned with form; with dividing and articulating space. In architecture color is used to emphasize the character of a building, to accentuate its form and material, and to elucidate its divisions.

If by "color" we mean not only the primary hues but also all the neutral tones from white through gray to black and all mixtures, then it is manifest that every building has color. What we are interested in here is its employment in a purely architectonic sense.

Originally, color was no problem at all; it came of itself. Man used the materials which Nature supplied and which experience taught him were strong and serviceable. The walls of his dwelling might be of hard-packed mud dug up on the building site or of stones gathered nearby. To these he added twigs, withes and straw. The result was a structure in nature's own colors, a human dwelling which, like a bird's nest, was an integral part of the landscape.

Primitive man decorated his neutral-colored wooden cot or adobe hut by festooning it with garlands of flowers or by covering the gray walls with colored fabrics. Thus he sought to improve on the rawness of nature, just as he might hang colorful ornaments on his sun-tanned body.

Later, man discovered how to make the materials more durable than they were from nature's hand, and new colors began to appear. By baking clay we get red and yellow bricks instead of the gray, sun-dried variety. By tarring wood we secure a deep black. Through such processes we are given a choice of several colors. As a rule, however, it is a limited one. The colors of bricks, for instance, lie within a rather narrow range. And even if the building materials are protected by a layer of paint, only a few colors can be depended on for strength and durability.

It is obvious that there is an inexplicable connection between materials and color. We do not experience color independently but only as one of several characteristics of a certain material. From the same yarn dyed with the same color can be made fabrics of very different character and the color will change with the texture. If, for instance, a glossy satin and a plush-like fabric are woven from the same silk, the first will be lustrous and light, the second will have depth and glow.

From the moment the color of building materials was controlled by man instead of produced by nature a new step in architectural design had been achieved. But human imagination seems to be very slow to grasp new possibilities. On the whole, we use the colors that we are accustomed to see around us. The dwelling is still part of the landscape. If there is yellow stone in the locality, the houses are very likely to be the yellow of that stone. And if they have plastered walls, it is sure to be yellow plaster derived from the local yellow sand. The window frames and shutters, however, may be painted a contrasting green or blue. In many civilizations the bright colors which are used are often separated by a white border which allows each color to stand forth in its full strength.

When we choose a color which is not determined by the building material itself, our choice will usually fall on one that is natural to some other material with which we are familiar. In contrast to their green surroundings, the log-houses in rural districts in Norway and Sweden are often painted a deep red. Today this is so generally the case that nobody notices it. But how did the custom originate? The Swedish art historian, Erik Lundberg, has advanced the theory that it started in imitation of the much grander and more durable red brick manor houses. The idea arose that a real house *had to be* red.

Later generations imitated stucco houses and their colors. On a Norwegian farm, where all the farm buildings have the old-fashioned coat of red, you are likely to find the house in Classic Revival. It, too, will be of wood but with a much finer finish: smooth boards painted in tones of gray and white or with delicate shades of yellow or rose, very reminiscent of the stucco houses of the period. But often stucco and wash colors are also imitations. In Italian towns they are usually the color of the local earth, as in Siena where the color of stucco houses is *terre di Siena*. But in other places you can find whitewashed walls with yellow plaster mouldings which are meant to resemble, or shall we say symbolize, sandstone.

It is probably simplifying the truth to call such employment of color "imitation." It is not an attempt to deceive people. Rather, the colors were regarded as symbols. On the whole, color, to most people, has always been highly symbolic. In Peking bright colors were reserved for palaces, temples and other ritual buildings. Ordinary dwellings were made colorless artificially; both brick and tile were subdued by means of a special baking process which made them as drab as road dust. Within the large precincts of the Temple of Heaven all roofs were of blue glazed tiles while the imperial palaces had yellow ochre roofs and the town gates green. Ordinary citizens were forbidden to use colored tiles.

Color is still used symbolically in many ways. There are special signal and warning colors; national, school and uniform colors; and colors for all sorts of clubs and societies. But quite apart from such use, there are colors which have a special meaning or which we reserve for definite purposes and occasions. Not only are cigars brown but their containers are made of brown wood, cedar or mahogany which best preserves the cigar and its bouquet. These cigar boxes with their white borders remind one of the houses mentioned above, with natural-colored walls accentuated by white trim. Very often the cigar box is ornamented with decoration in other material and color—gold and vivid hues printed on glossy paper. But regardless of how cigars are packed, we cannot imagine them in pink or mauve containers. We think of these colors more in connection with soap and perfumes, and they recall odors which are inimical to tobacco. We associate certain colors with masculine or feminine attributes. Thus, "tobacco" colors are suitable for the study, "perfumed" ones for the boudoir.

On the whole, it is difficult to fathom how we have come to associate certain colors with certain things. Foodstuffs, for instance, must all have their real colors. If we see them under a falsifying light, which changes their color, they become unappetizing. Certain colors have generally recognized psychological effects. Red, for example, is a fiery, exciting color; green is soothing. But many color conventions differ in different civilizations.

Correctly used, color may express the character of a building and the spirit it is meant to convey. While the aspect of one building should be light and gay, indicating festivity and recreation, another should have an austere and efficient look, indicating work and concentration. For both types there are colors which seem absolutely right and others which are entirely unsuitable.

By the use of a single color, or definite color scheme, it is possible to suggest the chief function of a building. But within the same building a variety of colors may be used to accentuate form, divisions and other architectonic elements. Certain colors can make an object seem lighter, others heavier, than it is. It can be made to appear large or small, near or distant, cool or warm, all according to the color it is given. There are innumerable rules and directives for the employment of color to hide blemishes and defects. Ugly structural parts can be "painted out" or made less obstructive. A small room can be made to appear larger by being given a pale color. Or if it is a cold room, with a northern or eastern exposure, it can be given artificial sunlight by being painted in warm tones, such as ivory, cream or peach. But there is something unsatisfactory about such camouflage. It is irritating

to discover that the thing is not what we expected. In good architecture, consciously designed, the small room appears small, the
large room large, and instead of disguising this it should be
emphasized by the judicious use of color. The small room
should be painted in deep, saturated tones so that you really feel
the intimacy of four walls closing about you. And the color scheme
of the large room should be light and airy to make you doubly
aware of the broad expanse from wall to wall.

A German theorist has described at length how color can be
used to emphasize not only what is large and what is small but
also what is up and what is down. The floor, he says, like the earth
we walk on should give an impression of gravity. Therefore it
should have the gray or brown tones of clay or rocky ground.
Walls, on the other hand, should have more color, like flowering
shrubs and trees and everything that rises above the solid earth.
And, finally, the ceiling should be light and airy, in tones of white
or delicate shades of pink and blue, like the sky over our heads.
It would give a feeling of insecurity, he claims, to walk on pink or
blue floors, and we would feel the ceiling as a heavy load weighing
us down if it were painted a dark color.

As I sit reading his rather theoretical explanation, I raise my
eyes from the book and gaze about the room. The floor is covered
with a Chinese rug in lovely indigo blue on which I walk every day
without the slightest feeling of insecurity.

I think of rooms I have seen in old manor houses with floors
of rose and gray marble, white-washed walls, and black beamed
ceilings so dark and heavy that you actually sense their weight.

Despite all theories we can say of color, as of all other elements
of architecture, that there are no definite rules, no directives
which, if followed closely, guarantee good architecture. Color can
be a powerful means of expression for the architect who has something to say. To one it may mean that the ceiling should be dark
and heavy, to another that it should be light and airy.

When man has reached the stage where he uses color not only
to preserve building materials and emphasize structure and tex-

tural effects, but to make a great architectural composition more clear, to articulate inter-relations between a series of rooms, then a great new field opens before him. In the Copenhagen city hall, from about 1900, the architect was so interested in all the technological details that he used color only to enhance the materials and to underline the building techniques. The result is that the rooms themselves seem to fall apart. You do not experience them as integrated wholes but only as a number of interesting details. The following generation of architects turned against this tendency, and in the Faaborg Museum (1912–14) Carl Petersen showed how the exactly opposite effect could be achieved by the correct use of color. Instead of emphasizing materials and structures, he used color to characterize the rooms themselves.

The octagonal domed hall in the museum was (as already mentioned above page 194) formed around Kai Nielsen's black statue of the founder, Mads Rasmussen. The walls are plastered, frescoed and polished so that their structure is completely hidden. The brickwork has not been allowed to distract attention from the room itself. The architect painted the walls a pure cobalt blue, which holds the octagon together. Carl Petersen grew up in the second half of the nineteenth century when subdued and broken colors were the fashion and bright colors were looked upon as inartistic and primitive. He attended a boarding school in which certain rooms were decorated in the Pompeian manner and one of his teachers, an old painter of an earlier generation, had in his home a room with cobalt blue walls. These colors made an indelible impression on the young schoolboy.

In the Faaborg Museum there is happy interplay between the dim illumination and the intense color of the domed hall. Pure colors become richer and more saturated when seen in half-light. Anyone who has seen mosaics in the solemn light of old churches will have experienced this. The cobalt blue in the museum hall would not be half so effective in brilliant sunlight. But here where the architect has consciously employed contrasting lighting effects, the color makes a fascinating background for the black stone statue.

It is generally believed that some colors are beautiful and others ugly, and that this holds good no matter how they are used. If this were true, the happy result obtained by Carl Petersen would have to be credited to the fact that he was lucky enough to find a number of beautiful colors and use them in his museum. But it is not as simple as that. Artists know that among the thousands of hues the human eye can distinguish, there is hardly one that would not be considered beautiful when used in the right combination and the right way. And, quite the reverse, there is no color which, in certain combinations, will not become exceedingly ugly.

It often happens that when an attractive color, seen on the walls of a particular room, is copied in another room it loses its attraction in the new surroundings. Indeed, the same color on the same surface may look very different when seen together with different colors. A neutral gray against a red surface will have a green tinge while against a green surface it will look decidedly red. And in a room with a window towards the south and one towards the north, the same gray wall will have a warm tone near the southern window and a cold one near the north.

Warm and cold colors play an important role in our lives and express very different moods and emotions. We experience them in the variations of daylight from morning to evening. It is true that the eye adjusts itself to the gradual change so that the local colors of details appear the same throughout the day. But if we observe the whole as a unit—a landscape or a street scene—we become aware of the changes in the color scheme. The entire mood changes with the changing light. This is most apparent in towns near the water where the atmosphere is moist. Walking along the shore of the Charles River in Boston, Massachusetts, in the early morning, you not only *feel* that the air is cool but you imagine that you can *see* it. Old buildings in Boston seem bright and new with sharply etched cool shadows, and scintillating gleams from sailing boats in the water make your eyes blink. But if you return to the same spot in the evening, just before sunset, you find the glaring colors of the morning now saturated and warm. The Hancock Building, which had stood gray-white and sharp against the morning sky, is now gold and red. The golden dome of the State House is seen floating in the Canaletto-like atmosphere as a second sun. You *feel* the warmth of the evening sun and you *see* its warm light.

If we imagine a large mansion with many rooms, we instinctively feel that the rooms must differ in character and color, even if they were all painted the same neutral whites and grays. There would be a number of cool rooms with a clear, bright light, and others that were warm and mellow and cosy. But from this we cannot conclude that the one set of rooms is better than the other from an æsthetic point of view. In the North the warm rooms would be preferred while in warmer climes the cool ones would be the choice. The cool atmosphere and clear tones of the northern rooms would be the most flattering to our possessions. We would hang our best paintings in those rooms.

Many good houses of the past have taken advantage of this difference in the character of their rooms. Monticello, designed by Jefferson as a French *maison de plaisance*, forms a good example. Facing the east is the entrance hall which is somewhat reminiscent of the cool outdoor architecture. From there you pass to the warmer living rooms of the house, facing west. The Virginian tradition called for a hall running straight through the house from east to west, with entrances at both ends to provide a consoling breeze on hot days. George Washington enriched this simple plan in his Mount Vernon home by adding a high-columned "piazza" towards the east. This created a cool, outdoor room overlooking the rolling landscape towards the Potomac, in lovely contrast to the west front which, with the kitchen annex and gardener's cottage, embraces the courtyard where the warm afternoon sun lingers. Inside the house, too, he utilized the qualities of daylight with great skill. The room he worked in is a library, compact and friendly with windows to the south, while the banquet hall, which is also one of his additions to the original building, is a lofty and airy room with a great Palladian window facing north.

When we recall such a building we remember it as a composition of many rooms of different character in which daylight and its colors play a decisive role. Instead of trying to make the cool rooms warm it is possible to do just the opposite by employing colors which emphasize their cool atmosphere. Even when the sun is warmest and most brilliant, daylight in northern rooms will have a blue undertone because all light here is, after all, solely and exclusively reflection from the sky. Blue and other cool colors show with great brilliance in northern rooms while warm colors show up poorly, as if seen under a lamp which sheds a bluish light. Therefore, if in northern rooms cool colors are used and in southern rooms warm colors, all of the colors will sparkle in their full radiance.

These conditions can be illustrated with the help of paintings by the two famous Dutch artists, Jan Vermeer and Pieter de Hooch. They both worked in Delft and both painted the same sort of interiors with people wearing the same costumes. They were contemporaries and lived quite near to each other. But nevertheless their paintings are as different as morning and evening. Vermeer represents the morning. His studio had a northern exposure out to the Voldergracht where the sun did not appear until late on summer afternoons—and at that time he apparently never painted for there is not a single sunbeam in one of his pictures. Pieter de Hooch painted his pictures in a house in Oude Delft where the rooms looked out on gardens towards the west, and he preferred the afternoon glow when the red sun poured in. The results in both cases were fully in keeping with the conditions they chose to work under. One depicts the beauty of cool light and cool colors, the other the charm of warm light and warm colors. By placing them side by side you discover that there is as much beauty in Vermeer's cool palette—the lavender blues and lemon yellows against a black and white tiled floor—as in the friendly good humor and warmth of Pieter de Hooch's browns and cinnabar reds.

CHAPTER X

Hearing Architecture

Can architecture be heard? Most people would probably say that
as architecture does not produce sound, it cannot be heard. But
neither does it radiate light and yet it can be seen. We see the light
it reflects and thereby gain an impression of form and material.
In the same way we hear the sounds it reflects and they, too, give
us an impression of form and material. Differently shaped rooms
and different materials reverberate differently.

We are seldom aware of how much we can hear. We receive a
total impression of the thing we are looking at and give no thought
to the various senses that have contributed to that impression. For
instance, when we say of a room that it is cold and formal, we
seldom mean that the temperature in it is low. The reaction prob-

Illustration above shows a scene from the motion picture The Third Man

ably arises from a natural antipathy to forms and materials found in the room—in other words, something we *feel*. Or it may be that the colors are cold, in which case it is something we *see*. Or, finally, it may be that the acoustics are hard so that sound—especially high tones—reverberate in it; something we *hear*. If the same room were given warm colors or furnished with rugs and draperies to soften the acoustics, we would probably find it warm and cosy even though the temperature was the same as before.

If we think it over, we shall find that there are a number of structures we have experienced acoustically. From my own childhood I remember the barrel-vaulted passage leading to Copenhagen's old citadel. When the soldiers marched through with fife and drums the effect was terrific. A wagon rumbling through sounded like thunder. Even a small boy could fill it with a tremendous and fascinating din—when the sentry was out of sight.

These early memories bring to mind the tunnel noises in the motion picture *The Third Man*. While the greater part of this picture is composed as a sort of collage of movie scenes and zither music which bears no relation to the action, the final scenes are entirely without music and give a very realistic visual and oral impression of a gangster hunt through the endless underground tunnels of Vienna's sewer system. The characteristic sounds which tunnels produce are clearly heard in the splashing of the water and the echoes of the men hunting the third man. Here, architecture is certainly heard. Your ear receives the impact of both the length and the cylindrical form of the tunnel.

Thorvaldsen's Museum in Copenhagen has an acoustical effect very much like that of passageways and tunnels. In 1834 the Danish king donated an old barrel-vaulted coach house to hold the works of the famous sculptor. The building was converted into a beautiful museum with one statue in each barrel-vaulted room, where the long echoes of the coach-house still seem to linger. It is a house for stone effigies and has none of the comforts of houses built for human beings. The floors are of stone, the walls of stone, the ceilings of stone, even the residents are of stone.

All of these hard, sound-reflecting surfaces give the rooms their hard, long-reverberating tones. When you enter this home of statues you are in a world that is very different from the rather provincial little capital of the nineteenth century which built it. It is more like Rome, great and dignified as the vaulted ruins of Antiquity or the stone corridors of the grandiose palazzos from which ease and comfort were debarred.

The energetic director of the museum employs many methods of attracting visitors, including music recitals among the works of art. The entrance hall is one of the noblest rooms in Copenhagen but certainly not designed for chamber music. It is necessary to convert the acoustics completely for these musical events by covering the floor with matting and hanging fabrics on the walls. Then, if the audience is large enough to compensate for the lack of upholstery in the austere hall the room changes its manners, gives up its stentorian voice and becomes so civilized that it is possible to distinguish every tone of each instrument.

This may lead to the opinion that the acoustics of Thorvaldsen's Museum are poor unless steps are taken to improve them— which is true enough when it is used for chamber music. But it could just as well be said that it has excellent acoustics, provided the right kind of music is performed. And such music exists. The chants that were created for the Early Christian church in Rome would sound very well in the stone hall of Thorvaldsen's Museum. The old basilicas were not vaulted but they had the same hard character with their mosaic floors, naked walls and marble columns. And they were so huge and empty that sound continued to reverberate in them back and forth between the massive walls. The greatest church of early Christendom was the Basilica of S. Peter, forerunner of the present Renaissance edifice in Rome. It was an enormous, five-aisled building with stone columns separating the aisles. In *Planning for Good Acoustics* Hope Bagenal explains why the acoustical conditions of such a church must by their very nature lead to a definite kind of music. When the priest wished to address the congregation he could not use his ordinary

M. G. Bindesbøll: Entrance hall, Thorvaldsen's Museum, Copenhagen

speaking voice. If it were powerful enough to be heard throughout the church, each syllable would reverberate for so long that an overlapping of whole words would occur and the sermon would become a confused and meaningless jumble. It therefore became necessary to employ a more rhythmic manner of speaking, to

Sectional drawing of the old S. Peter's basilica in Rome. From Alpharani
An idea of the size of the church can be obtained from the plan opposite which at one and
the same time shows the oblong race course from the time of Nero (furthest to left), the early
Christian basilica (center, hatched) and the Renaissance church which succeeded it (lighter tone)

recite or intone. In large churches with a marked reverberation there is frequently what is termed a "sympathetic note"—that is to say "a region of pitch in which tone is apparently reinforced." If the reciting note of the priest was close to the "sympathetic note" of the church—and Hope Bagenal tells us that probably both of them were, then as now, somewhere near A or A flat—the sonorous Latin vowels would be carried full-toned to the entire congregation. A Latin prayer or one of the psalms from the Old Testament could be intoned in a slow and solemn rhythm, carefully adjusted to the time of reverberation.

The priest began on the reciting note and then let his voice fall away in a cadence, going up and down so that the main syllables were distinctly heard and then died away while the others followed them as modulations. In this way the confusion caused by overlapping was eliminated. The text became a song which lived in the church and in a soul-stirring manner turned the

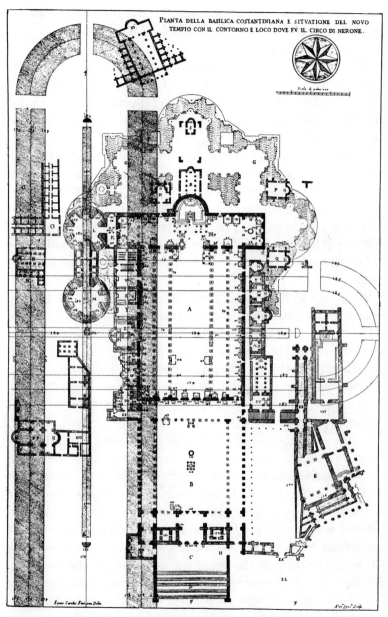

PLANTA DELLA BASILICA COSTANTINIANA E SITVATIONE DEL NOVO TEMPIO CON IL CONTORNO E LOCO DOVE FV IL CIRCO DI NERONE.

The old and the new S. Peter's, Rome. From Alpharani

great edifice into a musical experience. Such, for instance, are the Gregorian chants which were especially composed for the old basilica of S. Peter in Rome.

When this unison religious music heard on a gramophone record that was recorded in a studio with a comparatively short reverberation, is sounds rather poor. For, though too much overlapping causes confusion, a certain amount is necessary for good tone. Without it, choral music, especially, sounds dead. But when the same record is played in a room with long reverberations, the tone becomes much richer. The keynote is heard almost the entire time, gradually filling out and then withdrawing, and together with it the others are heard as intervals of a third or a fifth, so that the coinciding of notes produces a harmony as in part-singing. Thus, in the old churches the walls were in fact powerful instruments which the ancients learned to play upon.

When it was discovered that the unifying tonal effect of the church as an instrument was so great that more than one tone could be heard at the same time with pleasing results, the harmonies produced by the coinciding of notes began to be regulated and used. From this part-singing developed. "Polyphonic music, as heard today in Westminister Cathedral," says Hope Bagenal, "was directly produced by a building form and by the open vowels of the Latin language . . ."

Vaults, and more especially domed vaults, are acoustically very effective. A dome may be a strong reverberator and create special sound centers. The Byzantine church of S. Mark's, in Venice, is built over a Greek cross in plan and has five domes, one in the center and one over each of the four arms of the cross. This combination produces very unusual acoustical conditions. The organist and composer Giovanni Gabrieli, who lived around 1600, took advantage of them in the music he composed for the cathedral. S. Mark's had two music galleries, one to the right and one to the left, as far from each other as possible and each with its dome as a mighty resonator. The music was heard from both sides, one ans-

wering the other in a *Sonata Pian e Forte*. The congregation not
only heard two orchestras, it heard two domed rooms, one speaking with silver tones, the other responding in resounding brass.

Though this is a unique example, every large church interior has its own voice, its special possibilities. Hope Bagenal has convincingly demonstrated the influence of the historical types of church on schools of music and declamation. After the Reformation, changes affecting church acoustics had to be made in order to adapt the edifices for the new religion in which preaching in the native language played so important a role. Bagenal's analysis of the St. Thomas church at Leipzig, where Johan Sebastian Bach was the organist, is particularly interesting. Much of Bach's music was composed especially for that church. It is a large, three-aisled Gothic edifice with level vaults. After the Reformation large areas of resonant wood were added to the naked stone. The wood absorbed a great deal of sound and greatly reduced the period of reverberation. The side walls were lined with tiers of wooden galleries and numerous private boxes, or "swallow's nests," as they were called. The encroachment of so many boxes and galleries was due to the Lutheran system of church government which placed the church under the town council. Each member had his own family loge or box, just as one might at the opera. The new additions were in the Baroque style, with richly carved mouldings and panels, and there were curtains at the openings. Today, when the fixed rows of chairs on the floor and the gallery pews and boxes are filled, as they always are when Bach concerts are held, the congregation numbers about 1800. All this wood helped to create the acoustics that made possible the 17th century development of Cantata and Passion. Hope Bagenal figures the present reverberation at 2½ seconds as compared to from 6 to 8 seconds in the medieval church. The absence of a "note" or region of response in the church made it possible for Bach to write his works in a variety of keys.

These new conditions made possible a much more complicated music than could ever have been enjoyed in the early church.

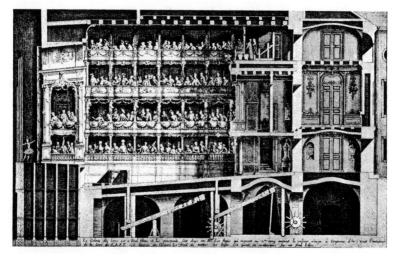

Sectional drawing of typical "loge" theater of 18th century

Bach's fugues, with their many contrapuntal harmonies, which would be lost in vast basilicas, could be successfully performed in St. Thomas's, just as the pure voices of the famous St. Thomas boys' choir receive full justice there.

St. Thomas Church, accoustically speaking, stands between the Early Christian church and the 18th century theater. In the latter, where tiers of loges or boxes covered the walls from floor to ceiling, there was even more sound absorption. The façades of the boxes were richly carved and the boxes themselves draped and upholstered. At each performance the floor was closely packed with a gala-clad audience. The ceiling was flat and relatively low so that it acted as a sounding-board, deflecting the tones in towards the boxes where they were absorbed by all the woodwork and upholstery. As a result, the reverberation was very short and every note—even in such florid musical ornaments as coloratura and pizzicato—could be distinctly heard.

In Copenhagen, in 1748, Nicolai Eigtved built the "Danish Comedy House" with an auditorium in the shape of a horseshoe and three tiers of boxes. In 1754 he designed a flat-roofed church

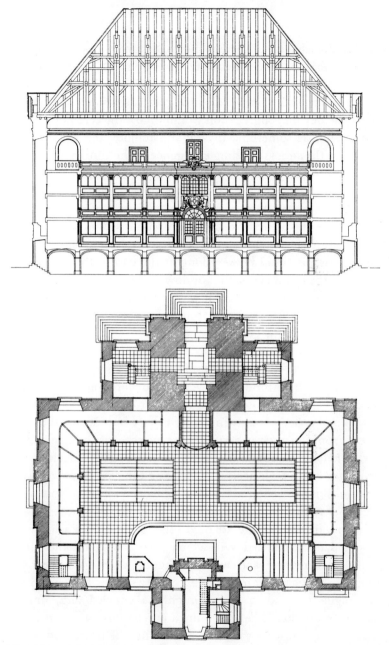

Nicolai Eigtved: Christian's Church, Christianshavn, Denmark. Section and plan, scale 1 : 400

for Christianshavn, just across the harbor from Copenhagen, in which galleries on three sides were formed almost like boxes in the theater. The entire interior was very foreign to any previous church tradition. Instead of sitting in a semidark nave from where the devout congregation would follow the ceremony at the distant altar as something mystic and remote, the worshippers here sat in the almost dazzling effulgence of the church of Rationalism, comfortably near the altar and pulpit. They were connected with, rather than separated from, the sacred ceremonies of their faith. It was a church in which the sermon was of major importance. Here, the preacher could really let himself go. If members of the congregation felt that his exhortation was too long-winded —and sermons could be *very* long at the end of the eighteenth century—they could close the windows in their pews and shut out all sound. This type of church was by no means unusual at the time. In Copenhagen alone four churches of similar type appeared during this period.

The Rococo period, which so radically created a new type of church to meet the requirements of a new age, also produced great town houses with interiors that were much more comfortable than those of the mansions of the Baroque period. The rooms in the new houses varied not only in size and shape but also in acoustical effect. From the covered carriage entrance the visitor came into a marble hall which resounded with the rattle of his sidearms and the clatter of his high heels as he followed the *major domo* across the stone floor and entered the door held open for him. Now came a series of rooms with more intimate and musical tones—a large dining room acoustically adapted for table music, a salon with silk- or damask-paneled walls which absorbed sound and shortened reverberations, and wooden dadoes which gave the right resonance for chamber music. Next came a smaller room in which the fragile tones of a spinet might be enjoyed and, finally, madame's boudoir, like a satin-lined jewelry box, where intimate friends could converse together, whispering the latest scandals to each other.

The Classic and Gothic revivals of the late eighteenth and early nineteenth centuries led inevitably to eclecticism in architecture in which creative design gave way to the accurate copying of details. Much that had been gained during the past centuries was first ignored and then forgotten. There was no longer any personal conception behind the rooms the architect planned and therefore he gave as little thought to their acoustic function and acoustical effect as to the texture of the materials he used. The exteriors of new churches were correct copies of Classic or Gothic prototypes but the interiors were not designed for definite types of oratory or music. In new theaters the flat ceilings of earlier days were discarded for slightly domed ceilings which produced acoustical conditions the architects could not master. Indifference to textural effects led to indifference to sound absorption. Even concert halls were designed quite casually, but as the programs they offered included every kind of music, with no regard for their special acoustical requirements, this was less important than it might have been. The height of confusion in this sense, however, came with the modern "talkies," in which you could see and hear the wide open prairie thundering under the hooves of galloping horses and at the same time listen to a symphonic orchestra playing romantic music à la Tschaikowsky—every possible banal effect served up in the same picture.

Radio transmission created new interest in acoustical problems. Architects began to study acoustical laws and learned how a room's resonance could be changed—especially how to absorb sound and shorten the period of reverberation. Too much interest has been given to these easily attained effects. The favorite interior of today seems to be something so unnatural as a room with one wall entirely of glass and the other three smooth, hard and shiny and at the same time with a resonance that has been so artificially subdued that, acoustically speaking, one might just as well be in a plush-lined mid-Victorian interior. There is no longer any interest in producing rooms with differentiated acoustical effects—they all sound alike. Yet the ordinary human being still enjoys variety, including variety of sound. For instance, a man tends to whistle or sing when he enters the bathroom in the morning. Though the room is small in volume, its tiled floor and walls, porcelain basin and water-filled tub, all reflect sound and reinforce certain tones so that he is stimulated by the resonance of his voice and imagines himself a new Caruso. What a flat feeling it gives when you come into a bathroom that has been given the favorite modern acoustical treatment which has the very one-sided aim of smothering all such cheerful noises. M. I. T.'s Faculty Club has one of the most perfectly equipped lavatories in the world. You enter it happily for a refreshing wash before lunch. A benefactor donated so much magnificent marble that it glistens with hard elegance and you say to yourself: "Here my voice is going to ring out marvellously." But the first joyous note from your lips falls as flat and muffled on your ear as it would in a heavily upholstered living-room. To put the finishing touch on this perfect marble washroom, the architect has given the ceiling the most sound-absorbing surface it is possible to attain!

I hope that I have been able to convince the reader that it is possible to speak of *hearing architecture*. Though it may be objected that, at any rate, you cannot hear whether or not it is good architecture, I can only say that neither is it certain you can *see* whether it is good or not. You can both see and hear if a building has character, or what I like to call *poise*. But the man has not yet been found who can pass judgment, logically substantiated, on a building's architectural value.

The only result of trying to judge architecture as you would a school paper—A for that building, B for that one, etc.—is to spoil the pleasure architecture gives. It is a risky business. It is quite impossible to set up absolute rules and criteria for evaluating architecture because every worthwhile building—like all works of art— has its own standard. If we contemplate it in a carping spirit, with a know-it-all attitude, it will shut itself up and have nothing to say to us. But if we ourselves are open to impressions and sympathetically inclined, it will open up and reveal its true essence.

It is possible to get as much pleasure from architecture as the nature lover does from plants. He cannot say whether he prefers the desert cactus or the swamp lily. Each of them may be absolutely right in its own locality and own clime. He loves all growing things, familiarizes himself with their special attributes and therefore knows whether or not he has before him a harmoniously developed example or a stunted growth of that particular variety. In the same way we should experience architecture.

Index

Index

Acknowledgments

The author is much indebted to Mrs. Imogen Cunningham, San Francisco, who took the photograph for the cover, and to Andreas Feininger for the frontispiece. The photograph on page 11 was taken by Mogens Amsnæs, Copenhagen; pp. 19, 21, 30, and 31 by Jonals Co, Copenhagen; p. 22 by Eric de Maré, London; pp. 23, 56, 58, 63, 64, 65, 69, 73 by Anderson, Rome; p. 25 by Villy Svarre, Aarhus; p. 34 by Vagn Hansen, Copenhagen; p. 51 by Sune Sundahl, Stockholm; on p. 54 both photographs are from Novico, Copenhagen; p. 97 by Professor Nils Ahrbom, Stockholm; p. 127 by Politikens Presse Foto, Copenhagen; p. 130 by Alinari, Rome; p. 149 by Farabola, Milan; pp. 155, 157, 158, 184 are from the News Service, M.I.T.; p. 163 from General Motors Corporation; p. 179 by Witherington Studios, London; p. 227 by F. Hendriksen, Copenhagen. A number of pictures are of uncertain origin, and the author has not been able to identify them. Appreciation is herewith rendered to the unknown photographers. The majority of photographs are by the author.